MW00901269

Business 101 Workbook

Marketing, Finance and Accounting

A learning workbook program for students 9 years old and beyond.

Visit the Y.M.B.A. website at www.YMBAgroup.com

ISBN-13: 978-1505552591
ISBN-10: 1505552591

Printed by CreateSpace, An Amazon.com Company.
Available at Amazon.com, www.YMBAgroup.com and other retail outlets.
CreateSpace, Charleston, SC

Consult a professional when seeking advice and making decisions. This is a learning book discussing
topics in a general style, not intended to be considered professional advice, suggestions or guidance.

Submit all inquiries at the website www.YMBAgroup.com

Y.M.B.A. Marketing - grades 4 5 6 7 8 + ages 9 10 11 12 13 14 +

Business 101 - Workbook

Marketing, Finance and Accounting

This page intentionally left blank.

THE YOUTH M.B.A. GROUP - BUSINESS 101 WORKBOOK
MARKETING, FINANCE AND ACCOUNTING
TABLE OF CONTENTS

This page intentionally left blank.

Y.M.B.A. educational series is designed with students 9 years old and beyond in d. This learning textbook teaches both useful life skills and college course topics in a olified style to encourage interest and learning. A single topic is presented at a time in a ailed and simple to understand format. Ideas are approached in a variety of styles to capture ariety of student learning styles.

iness concepts are generally introduced to students at the end of high school or in college. .B.A. believes students can achieve an understanding of the business world with the use of oyable introduction based lessons. Y.M.B.A. topics are discussed using relevant examples that based on familiar student scenarios.

ch Y.M.B.A. book includes a summary of incorporated practice skills. The distribution of practice as is indicated by the number below the respective practice skill learning tile. This learning tbook has a sample of the learning categories found within each Y.M.B.A. learning workbook. ch book balances the lesson concepts with the use of fun examples to enhance student interest.

aluating business decisions and building life skills establish a foundation for learning the business ects of any profession in the future. Business skills are utilized in every industry and an derstanding of business is essential for future success. So why wait? Begin achieving more h Y.M.B.A. learning workbooks and provide a path for future accomplishment.

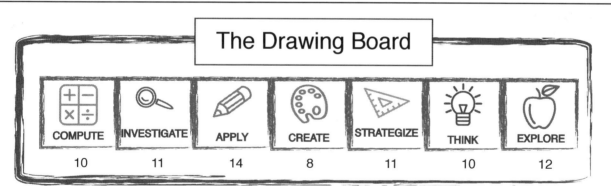

The Drawing Board

COMPUTE	INVESTIGATE	APPLY	CREATE	STRATEGIZE	THINK	EXPLORE
10	11	14	8	11	10	12

you selected the learning workbook to accompany this textbook the pages will advance together. or example, page 12 in the learning textbook will have a partner worksheet on page 12 of the arning workbook. The worksheet pages, known as "The Drawing Board", provide an opportunity r students to implement the details of the most recent lesson. The worksheets reinforce the lesson the student applies the learned skills using reasoning and analysis. This pattern keeps students ngaged and actively learning with the use of on-going student input.

ach workbook includes an end of book quiz to provide students a chance to demonstrate their hanced understanding of the subject. As the student completes the learning workbook you ill likely see a demonstration of pride and confidence in their new life and business skills.

MARKETING

The Drawing Board

Imagine you are an inventor.

A friend challenges you to make a new product. The only materials you may use are:

screws	glue	fabric
wood	wheels	paper

You may use as much or as little of each of these materials as you choose. You may also choose to use only some of the materials. You will create your new product in a workshop that has all the tools you need.

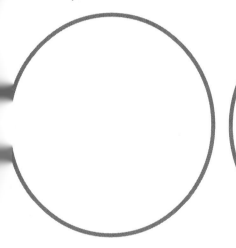 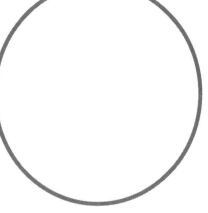 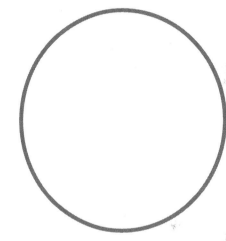

Invention Front View   Invention Top View   Invention Back View

Consider the following questions:

1. What did you name your invention? _____

2. What does your invention do? What are the benefits? _____

_____

3. What consumers do you think will buy your invention? _____

4. Will the marketing of the invention focus on a product benefit,
   a product feature or a limited time sale? _____

EXPLORE

9

Imagine you are the owner of an ice cream shop.

Last Tuesday at 9:00 in the morning your ice cream delivery company arrived. At the same time your vendor arrived to re-fill your juice machine. The ice cream delivery worker wheel in a cart of one flavor, then returned to his truck to get the next flavor. This was the usual pa every Tuesday for the ice cream delivery ... and your shop offers 28 flavors! The juice mac vendor began his delivery following the same path for the juice re-fills, one juice at a time.

Swish! Plop! Whoop! Plunk! The ice cream delivery person was bringing in the mango ic cream and the juice company delivery person was bringing in the grape juice. One slipped and the other tripped and then both fell to the floor. The mango ice cream mixed with the grape soda .. and smelled yummy! You try a scoop and a new invention was discovered!

MANGO GRAPE

Create your ad in the space below for the local newspaper to tell of the new ice cream fla

CREA

Every good or service that is purchased uses a type of marketing to let potential customers know about the product. List any products that you choose below and include in the next box why that product needs marketing.

Product	Why Does It Need Marketing?
Hotel	To show travelers the beautiful hotel so they want to visit.

Consider different careers in marketing. Select one career and fill in the space below answering the questions: Which career did you choose? What part do you think would be enjoyable? Why is this job needed in a company?

_____

_____

_____

_____

_____

_____

_____

_____

_____

_____

_____

THINK

The Drawing Board

Build The Plan

CircusPals, Inc. would like your help. The new face paint product is being developed and prepared for sale. The company is looking for new ideas to use in the marketing and advertising.

Fill in the blanks in each of the circles below to help the company develop the face paint product marketing plan.

Who Is The Target Customer That Will Buy The Product?

_____

Where would you market (advertise) the CircusPals face paint?

_____

What is one benefit to advertise of the product?

_____

Face Paint

Which retail store would sell a face paint product?

_____

Similar face paint sells for $5 – $15. What price do you suggest?

_$____

What month of year will see the highest face paint sales?

_____

CREATE

The Drawing Board

Make A Cash Cow

hen a company is bringing a new product to market the hope
hat the product will be an instant success. If marketing is
:cessful and many customers buy the product it can be a cash
w for the company. "Cash Cow" is another way of saying a
·y successful product that earns the company a high profit.

products take the dedication and hard work of a team of people.
metimes parts of the marketing plan need to be changed, or
rected, to help increase the chance for a products success.

ted below is a product name, features of the product and the price of the product.
 the last column circle which part of the marketing plan you believe was a problem,
d therefore a part of the reason the product did not succeed.

Product Name	Special Features	Price	Problem
Zip Color Crayons	Crayons where every line makes a rainbow of color.	$2.00	Poor Product Name Price Too High Poor Product Idea
Splash Water Light	Waterproof reading light for the bathtub.	$9.00	Poor Product Name Price Too High Poor Product Idea
3. Bark Bites	Organic dog food treats.	$24.00	Poor Product Name Price Too High Poor Product Idea
4. Sweat Sneakers	Sneakers with special stay-dry material that does not get wet.	$29.95	Poor Product Name Price Too High Poor Product Idea
Vitamin Chocolate	A chocolate bar with vitamins.	$14.95	Poor Product Name Price Too High Poor Product Idea

6. Select one of the products listed above in the chart. What would you suggest as a correction to the problem? What can the company do to improve the marketing?

_____

_____

_____

_____

_____

_____

INVESTIGATE

www.YMBAgroup.com

Royal Sports Company is a successful sports equipment company. The company manufactures and sells over 42 different sports balls. The company goal is to keep looking for new ways to improve the products. The company knows the produ improvements will encourage buyers to stay loyal to the Royal Sports equipment brand. The Royal Sports customers seek the most up-to-date product on the market. To stay a customer favorite Royal Sports has a research team to develop new marketing ideas that help ensure a product is what a buyer wants or needs.

Technology

Buyer Habits

Changes That Create A Need For An Updated Marketing Plan

Competition

Government Laws

Royal Sports inventors just announced a new fabric for tennis balls. The new fabric on the tennis ball makes a ball glow at night. Another benefit of the new fabric is that the ball can hold in the air longer so it will bounce longer. The price will increase .89 cents a ball. Players can now play tennis into night. What are some sales bursts Royal Sports can add to the tennis ball package?

New Improved Flavor

More Colors Available!

APPLY

The Drawing Board

Imagine You Are Shopping For A New TV.
~~ce in order the eight customer buying expectations shown at the bottom of the page.
~would be the most important to you in a TV purchase, 8 would be the least important.

1. _____

2. _____

3. _____

4. _____

5. _____

6. _____

7. _____

8. _____

MOST IMPORTANT

LEAST IMPORTANT

A goal of marketing research
is to find new ideas to help a
company build a relationship between
the business and the customer.

Eight Points A Customer Expects When Buying A Product

To Work As Advertised   Useful Features

Extended Warranty   Fair Price

Easy Return Process   Friendly Service

Helpful Instructions   Color and Size Options

EXPLORE

15

How many different competitor brands can you list for each of the following products

Sneakers: _____ _____ _____

Cereal: _____ _____ _____

Cars: _____ _____ _____

Toys: _____ _____ _____

Hotels _____ _____ _____

Gas Stations: _____ _____ _____

Direct Competitor
Grocery Store -> Grocery Store

Indirect Competitor
DVD Movie Retail Store -> DVD Rental

Retail stores are direct competitors with each other retail stores.

Inside retail stores you find brands that are direct competitors with other brands

Look at the words below found on an updated products package
Circle which one is most likely to capture your attention.

Buy Me	I'm The Best	I Have A Low Price

I Have A Fancy Box	Earn Rewards!

STRATEGIZ

The Drawing Board

sted below numbered one to ten are possible purchases by a customer. Write in the
lank GOOD, SERVICE or BOTH depending on if the consumer is buying a good, buying
 service or buying a good and service at the same time.

1. A volleyball net from an internet website. _____

2. Pizza served at a restaurant._____

3. Annual teeth cleaning by a dentist. _____

4. Crayons from a catalog in the mail. _____

5. Printer ink for your home printer from the office supply store. _____

6. Pet food for your dog from the veterinarian at the exam. _____

7. Exercise weights from at a sports equipment store. _____

8. A custom imprinted award for your soccer coach. _____

9. A bounce house rental to be installed in the backyard Sunday. _____

10. Making a deposit into your savings account at your bank. _____

Marketing In Action

1. What is one good you saw someone purchase this past week?

2. What is one service you saw someone purchase this past week?

3. What is an example of a time when you or a family member
   purchased a good and a service at the same time?

THINK

17

Congratulations! You just became the manager at ASA-Country. ASA-Country is a clothing store focused on young adults 18-35 years old. In general, the customers who shop in the store buy 50% womens clothes, 25% accessories, 20% mens clothes and 5% clothes in the childrens department. Your regional manager has asked for your ideas on the store floor plan. Reminder, consider ideas that will make the store helpful to customers so they stay and shop!

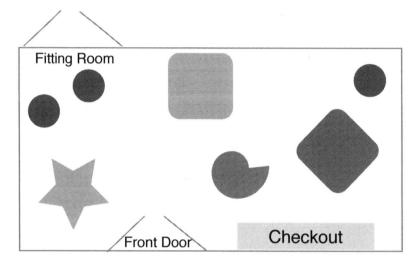

1. Why does the manager have the clearance discount racks in the back of the store?

2. The regional manager has placed the womens clothes section across the store from the fitting room and away from the babies and kids section. What suggestions do you have on how this layout can be improved?

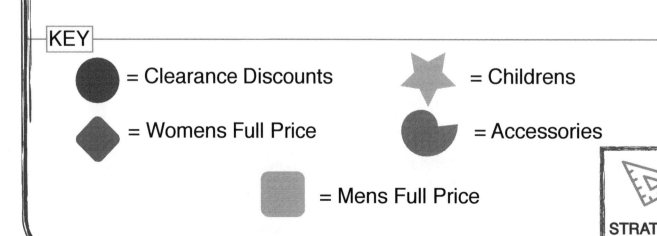

KEY

= Clearance Discounts   = Childrens

= Womens Full Price   = Accessories

= Mens Full Price

STRATEGIZE

Look who just received a gift in the mail! Inside the wrapped box is an alarm clock. The alarm clock features are listed below. Design what you imagine the outside of the alarm clock box would have as a design. Use some or all of the details below in the design.

Be sure to include the company name and price on the box. What other details would be on the clock box to encourage buyers to purchase? How does the box design catch a buyers attention?

Alarm Clock Details

Brand Name: ClockTown USA, Inc.
Colors: Black, Blue, White
Price: $14.95
Power: Plug or Battery

Feature: Large, Easy Read Numbers
Feature: Two Different Alarm Sounds
Feature: $3 Coupon Off Batteries Inside
Feature: Small Design, Easy For Travel

Alarm Clock
Box Front View

CREATE

A Nice Price

Below is a list of common products. Imagine that you are the price manager at The Rapid Shop Company. Your task today is to set a price for each of these items. The goal of the price is for it to be one that the customer will find most appealing. At which price is the customer most likely to buy the product?

Hint: The most eye-catching price is not always the lowest price.

	Product	Most Eye-Catching Consumer Price		
1.	1 bag of potato chips	80¢	74¢	75¢
2.	1 medium pizza	$4.95	$4.80	$4.97
3.	2 baseballs	99¢	$1.00	90¢
4.	2 ice cream cones	98¢	88¢	95¢
5.	10 pencils	49¢	47¢	50¢
6.	4 notebooks	$4.95	$4.92	$4.97
7.	3 cookies	99¢	96¢	98¢
8.	1 jump rope	80¢	72¢	75¢
9.	6 strawberries	86¢	89¢	90¢
10.	8 balloons	$5.55	$5.56	$5.53

11. How many prices above did you circle that end with the numbers 5 or 9? _____

12. Review the prices you circled above. How many were the lowest of the three prices being considered on the line? _____

13. Why do you think you did not circle the lowest price on each row?

_____

_____

APPLY

Public Relations

A company has an image in the marketplace. The image is how the potential customers view the company. Company loyalty is when a customer is dedicated to a specific brand or company. This loyalty may be based on national charity events or local community areas where the company provides assistance.

1. What are some ways a company can offer help in a community?

2. What can a company do to keep current customers happy?

3. How could a business lend a hand when urgent help is needed?

4. What marketing can a business use to keep the company name in the mind of potential customers in a community?

The Brand Logo

A brand logo is a picture or design that customers identify with a specific company. Look around the room and identify a company logo or brand name. Make a list in the blanks below. Find ten and you are a logo super star!

1.   6.

2.   7.

3.   8.

4.   9.

5.   10.

INVESTIGATE

1. Is each product below a buyer need or want?
Circle each need. Underline each want.

Water
Puppy Dog
Bottled Water
Medicine
Scented Shampoo
Notebook With A Sparkle Cover
Designer Medicine Case
Bar of Soap
Video Game
A Place To Live

When A "Need" Becomes A "Want"

Did you know a company will try to convince a customer that something they "want" is something that they "need"?

2. Imagine you are shopping for hand soap. Generally you purchase the store brand at $1.49 for two bars of soap. While in the store, you see a display in the isle that catches your attention. The soap company, Sudzy, is offering three bars of new lemon luxury scented soap for $2.79. What would some buyers do and why?

Determine if the buyer situation below is an **urgent need to buy** or **time to shop**.

3. You start a new job tomorrow and need a suit. _____

4. It is 8:00 p.m. you need to feed your dog and are out of dog food. _____

5. Next month you are taking a vacation and need a bathing suit. _____

6. Thanksgiving decorations just began to be placed out in stores.
You need shoes for New Years Eve. _____

EXPLORE

A.I.D.A.

2
Interest

1
Attention

3
Desire

4
Action

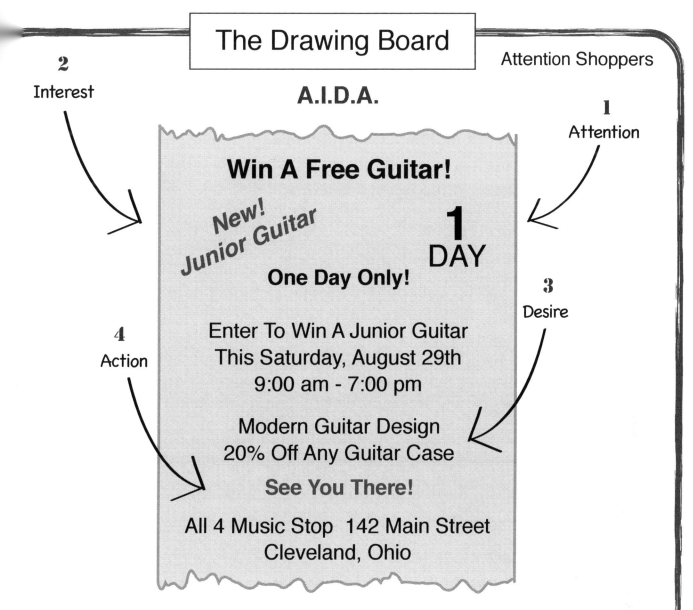

Win A Free Guitar!

New! Junior Guitar

1 DAY

One Day Only!

Enter To Win A Junior Guitar
This Saturday, August 29th
9:00 am - 7:00 pm

Modern Guitar Design
20% Off Any Guitar Case

See You There!

All 4 Music Stop 142 Main Street
Cleveland, Ohio

Imagine you are the manager at Cookies Chip Shop. A new cookie named the Pizza Cookie is being first offered for sale on October 1 at the local County Fair.

1. What would you write in the advertisement to catch a customers "Attention"?

2. What would you write to keep the "Interest" of a buyer?

3. What would you write to increase the "Desire" in a buyer for the product?

4. What would you write to encourage a buyer to take "Action"?

APPLY

A marketing plan needs to be aware of the current life cycle stage of a product. This will help a company make marketing decisions that better meet potential customer needs and wants. Responding to these needs and wants in a marketing message will help a company attract buyers.

1. What are two promotion ideas that may be used when introducing a new product?

_____

2. Why do you think products are not able to always be in the "moving" stage?

_____

3. At the "maximum" stage the product has the most customer demand. When there is a lot of customer demand the product price will increase. At the "maximum" stage is it likely or unlikely coupons will be offered for the product? Why?

_____

4. During the "minimizing" stage customer demand for the product goes down. Since there is less demand for the product what do you think will happen to the price?

_____

5. A change in technology may be a reason for a product to enter the "exit" stage of the life cycle. What is one product that was no longer demanded (needed) by the customer due to a change in technology? _____

_____

6. Two years ago 10,000 happy shirts were sold. Last year 7,000 happy shirts were sold. This year it is expected that 4,000 happy shirts will be sold. What stage of the product life cycle does this describe? _____

7. Hot-Z Fitness Gym opened last year. The gym already has 85 more members than the competitor. What stage of the product life cycle does this describe? _____

8. Flight Weight Company just spent $18,000 in radio advertisements in the Northeast to tell customers about their new product, travel size exercise weights. What stage of the product life cycle does this describe?

EXPLORE

Leading Questions and Non-Leading Questions

Non-leading questions are important to gathering useful marketing research. Below are four survey questions. Circle each question to show if it is leading or non-leading.

1. Everyone adores the new sandwich shop in town. Do you think they like it?

        Leading   Non-Leading

2. Rate how much you enjoy the tomato soup. 1 for not much, 10 for very much.

        Leading   Non-Leading

3. Up to 10, how many stars would you give the waitress at your table today?

        Leading   Non-Leading

4. How do you think the restaurant is kept so clean?

        Leading   Non-Leading

Open Ended Questions and Closed Questions

Open ended questions encourage a detailed answer. Closed questions only seek a one word answer. There are not many details learned from closed end questions. When a company is trying to understand potential customers more detailed answers are more helpful. Open ended questions give more information to market researchers.

5. Did you try the new fresh baked bread?

        Open Ended   Closed

6. How could we have better served you today?

        Open Ended   Closed

7. In your opinion, was your lemonade cold?

        Open Ended   Closed

8. Why did you choose to visit here today?

        Open Ended   Closed

APPLY

The Drawing Board

A company uses marketing to sell a product. A product may be either a good, a service or both a good and a service. Shown below are business names. Indicate if the product the business will sell is likely to be a good, a service or both. In the last column write what you think may be one product sold by the company.

Company Name	Good, Service, or Both	Product Sold
1. Music Mania Co.	_____	_____
2. The Icing Shop	_____	_____
3. United Gas Station	_____	_____
4. Pizzaz Magic Shop	_____	_____
5. Sparkle Nail Spa Co.	_____	_____
6. Regal Bank, LLC	_____	_____
7. Boating Fun Company	_____	_____
8. Reds Auto Repair Co.	_____	_____

THINK

bank teller	waitress	landscaper	insurance agent
sports coach	carpet installer	fitness trainer	hair stylist

Select a service industry job shown in the box above. Next, design a newspaper advertisement below for the local paper. The goal of the advertisement is to get the attention of new potential customers. Before you begin consider who your target customer will be and what you company is looking to sell.

Be sure to include the 4 P's of marketing in the advertisement.

Product, Place, Promotion and Price

Who is the target potential customer that you hope will visit your location after seeing the advertisement?

_____

CREATE

Decision Scenarios

Listed below are four marketing questions to consider. Using full sentences write your answers below.

1. Bon Yummie Incorporated is your favorite restaurant. To appreciate you as a return customer the head chef notices your reservation and prepares a special meal. The food you are paying for is a "good". But the restaurant also provides services. What are some services provided by the restaurant?

2. Imagine you are at TV-Pa-Looza, Inc. where you work as the repair manage Last month the store repaired 42 televisions. Next month the store expects twice as many customers. How many televisions should you expect to repair?

3. Chilly 'N Cold, LLC is a service company, but when a customer needs a part of the air conditioner replaced the company will also sell the replacement item. Although the company sells parts for products it is known as a service company. Why is Chilly 'N Cold be called a service company and not a goods company?

4. Tropical Tours, Inc. is a resort hotel. The hotel offers a shark experience tour for the guests. Why would it be important for Tropical Tours to have excellent customer service when selling the shark experience tour?

STRATEGIZE

The Drawing Board

CUSTOMER	PLACE	PROMOTION	SALE
GOOD	PRICE	RESEARCH	SERVICE
MARKET	PRODUCT	RETAIL	STORE

Complete the word search below. Find all the words n the word box above.

```
N  G  O  O  D  J  I  Z  V  E
P  R  O  M  O  T  I  O  N  V
K  P  L  A  C  E  I  A  R  P
M  A  R  K  E  T  P  E  E  R
P  R  I  C  E  R  M  C  S  E
F  U  V  B  O  O  S  I  E  T
F  V  Z  D  T  T  E  V  A  A
L  K  U  S  O  L  B  R  R  I
E  C  U  R  A  A  U  E  C  L
T  C  E  S  P  H  Z  S  H  R
```

Unscramble the following words. Use the word box at the top of the page for clues.

1. TIELRA   _____

2. REMKAT   _____

3. ALPCE   _____

4. CIPRE   _____

5. ELSA   _____

INVESTIGATE

29

The Drawing Board

Pick A Market

Identify the target market. Draw a line from the product in the left column to the likely target market in the right column. Remember, a target market is the group of buyers being advertised toward that is most likely to purchase a product.

Product	Target Market
Two-2-Go Baby Stroller	Target Market: Age 20-40 Location: National Interest: New Parents
Fitness Restore Health Water	Target Market: Age 20-40, Female Location: National Interest: Team Sports
Fresh Sports Flower Scented Bags	Target Market: Age 20-40 Location: National Interest: Fitness
Pet360 Handy Vacuum	Target Market: Age 40-60 Location: National Interest: Crafts
Ciz-Or Fabric Cutters	Target Market: Age 20-40 and 40-60 Location: North USA Interest: Winter Sports
365 Solar Sun Glasses	Target Market: Age 20-40 and 40-60 Location: National Interest: Animals
Rugged Turf Snow Boots	Target Market: Age 15-20 and 20-40 Location: South USA Interest: Outdoors

APPLY

Copyright Protected. 30 www.YMBAgroup.com

Select your favorite toy or hobby. Imagine a company that sells the toy contacted you to ask for a new idea for a commercial. Below is a storyboard for the commercial that will be 30 seconds in length. Each square in the series represents 5 seconds of time in the commercial. First sketch a picture of what is happening in the scene. Next, below the box write a few words to describe the scene.

What is the product? _____

Who is the target market for this product? _____

<table>
<tr><td></td><td></td><td></td></tr>
</table>

<table>
<tr><td></td><td></td><td></td></tr>
</table>

CREATE

Refer to the Simple Sales Statement for Wayve Surf Shop and answer the following questions in the space provided.

1. What is the total amount of company gross sales at Wayve Surf Shop? _____

2. What is the total amount of net sales after the returns and discounts? _____

3. The cost of goods sold is the total amount the company had to spend to have the product available to sell. This would include surf boards, sun tan lotion, bathing suits, and all the other products for sale in the store. How much did the company spend on products to sell between January 1, 2014 and December 31, 2014?

4. The company has 2 employees, each paid the same amount. Payroll is included in the operating expenses. At the surf shop payroll is 50% of operating expenses. What did one employee earn in payroll during 2014?

After the company paid all the bills the money that remains is left is called profit. The profit is the money when there are no bills currently due to be paid. The profit of a business may be used for a number of purposes. A business goal is to grow. The profit that is in the bank after all costs are paid gives the business the ability to grow and expand. Updates to a business may include product updates, hiring new employees growing an existing marketing program or updating employee uniforms.

The Wayve Surf Shop Company
Simple Sales Statement
01/01/2014 - 12/31/2014

Gross Sales	$82,000
Less: Returns	$ 2,500
Less: Sales/Discounts/Coupons	$ 9,000
Net Sales	$70,500
Less: Cost of Goods Sold	$25,500
Less: Operating Expenses	$42,400
Net Income	$ 2,600

COMPUTE

Find The Sale Price

Pet-A-Torium, Inc. is celebrating 20 years in business and as a thank you to customers the store is having a big sale! Compute the sale prices below.

Pet-A-Torium

Celebrating 20 Years Of *Woof*-Tastic Customers! We *Tank* You. *Fin*-ish Your Day At Our Store. You Will *Meow* At The Sale Prices!

---

1. Product: *Kitten Toys*

Current Price: $5.00

Sale Discount: 40 %

Sale Price: $ 3.00

Show Your Work in This Column
(1) Change percent to decimal 40$ = .4
(2) Multiply $5.00 x .4 = $2.00 to know sale discount
(3) Subtract the full price from the sale discount
   $5.00 – $2.00 = $3.00
$3.00 is the sale price for the kitten toys.

---

2. Product: *Hamster Food*

Current Price: $7.99

Sale Discount: 10 %

Sale Price: $

---

3. Product: *Rabbit Hutch*

Current Price: $85.00

Sale Discount: 25 %

Sale Price: $

---

4. Product: *Puppy Beds*

Current Price: $19.95

Sale Discount: 30 %

Sale Price: $

---

5. Product: *Bird Cages*

Current Price: $59.95

Sale Discount: 20 %

Sale Price: $

COMPUTE

The Drawing Board

Answer the questions below in the space provided using the budget below.

Wayve Surf Shop Company	2014 Budget	2014 Actual	2014 Variance	2015 Budget
Revenue				
Gross Sales Revenue	69,000	70,100	2,100	75,500
Less: Returns	200	400	400	500
Net Sales Revenue	68,800	70,500	1,700	75,000
Expenses				
Advertising	8,000	8,500	(500)	9,000
Electric	3,000	3,200	(200)	3,400
Inventory	25,500	25,500	0	23,500
Office Supplies	3,500	3,600	(100)	3,800
Payroll	21,200	21,200	0	28,000
Repairs	4,000	4,200	(200)	1,000
Telephone	1,700	1,700	0	1,700
Total Expenses	65,900	67,900	2,000	70,400
Net Income	2,900	2,600	(300)	4,600

| In 2013 the best guess for 2014 results. | The actual 2014 sales and expenses. | The difference between the best guess and actual. | In 2014 the best guess for 2015 results. |

1. Wayve Surf Shop Company has decided to budget $75,500 in net sales for 2015. Looking at the budget data, is this a reasonable goal? Explain your answer.

2. In what three categories did the company spend the same amount as budget?

3. What two categories are planned to be the largest expenses in 2015?

4. (a) What is the total amount spent on inventory in 2014? _____

   (b) What are the total net sales in 2014? _____

   (c) Using these two pieces of information, how much did the company earn in sales above the inventory cost? (known as the mark-up)

   _____

COMPUTE

FINANCE

The Drawing Board

Match the term with the word it is describing. If you are unsure of a word use dictionary to find the meaning. Draw a line to the definition in the next column.

asset

stock

investor

merger

interest rate

acquisition

return

profit

earnings

Person who gives money in the hope that the company will return the amount, plus extra money called interest.

A company sales less expenses equals the money the company made in the business.

Company 1 and company 2 come together and may create new company 3.

An item of value that is owned and is cash or may be sold for cash.

The amount of money earned on an investment usually paid monthly or annually.

Purchased by shareholders who want to own a part of the corporation.

Company 1 takes over company 2 and only company 1 continues to exist.

The amount of money an investment returns to an investor, a percent.

The money earned by an investor after expenses and fees are deducted.

EXPLORE

The Drawing Board

Barter System Conversions

TOOL BOX

1 Red Bead = 2 Brown Beads
2 Brown Beads = 1 Chicken
3 Chickens = 1 Goat

2 Goats = 1 Cow
2 Cows = 1 Horse
4 Horses = 1 Wagon

1 Red Bead = $2.50   2 Brown Beads = $5

Based On the Information Above: The cost in dollars an cents for each item.

Red Bead equals 2 Brown Beads = $5.00
Brown Beads is $10.00 = 1 Chicken
Chickens is $30.00 = 1 Goat

2 Goats is $60.00 = 1 Cow
2 Cows is $120 = 1 Horse
4 Horses are $480 = 1 Wagon

Now look at the items picked up on a trip to the market 200 years ago.
Write the total spent on the trip on the line next to each list.

$ _____

6 chickens
2 cows
1 goat

4. $ _____

1 chicken
1 horse

$ _____

2 horses
1 wagon

5. $ _____

8 goats
2 wagons

$ _____

4 cows
8 chickens

6. $ _____

1 cow
1 goat
1 wagon

COMPUTE

The Drawing Board

Future demand can be predicted generally reliably since it grows at a consistent, predictable rate. The reason for the consistent growth of demand is because the population of people in a country or marketpla also grows at a predictable rate.

Plot the annual population of Diversifyatopia on the graph below. The first item of data has been completed as shown by the star.

(1977, 1 million)   (1992, 2.5 million)
(1982, 1.5 million)   (1997, 3 million)
(1987, 2 million)   (2002, 3.5 million)

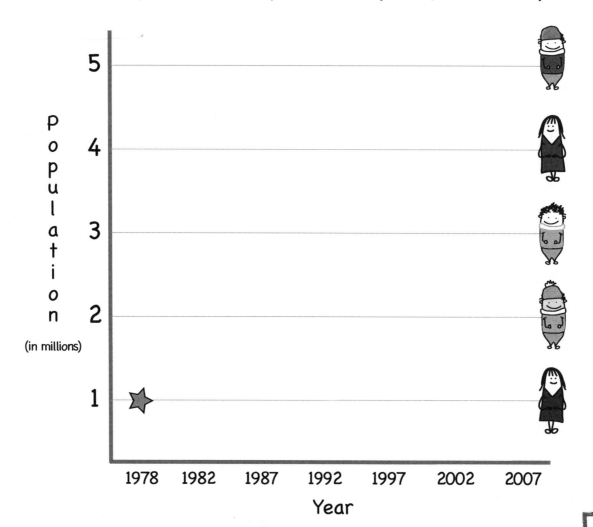

1. Based on the data and the graph, what do you think the population of Diversifyatopia was in the year 2007? _____ million people.

INVESTIGAT

The Drawing Board

Select the best answer for the true and false questions below. If you select false, circle the word that is not correct the write the word that would more correctly belong in the sentence.

1. Increasing the number of shoppers and sellers create a need for less jobs.

   True   False, the correct word is _____

2. The goal of the F.D.I.C. is to ensure pencils are available to bank customers.

   True   False, the correct word is _____

3. The F.D.I.C. headquarters is located in Albany, New York.

   True   False, the correct word is _____

4. The abbreviation F.D.I.C. stands for Fun Deposit Insurance Corporation.

   True   False, the correct word is _____

5. The government doesn't want people to save money in a bank.

   True   False, the correct word is _____

6. A bank uses diamonds deposited from customers to loan to other customers.

   True   False, the correct word is _____

7. One goal of the F.D.I.C. is to make envelopes available to banks.

   True   False, the correct word is _____

8. A second goal of the F.D.I.C. is to assist the bank in painting.

   True   False, the correct word is _____

9. The F.D.I.C. is managed by eight people who are approved by Congress.

   True   False, the correct word is _____

10. The idea for the F.D.I.C. came after the financial troubles in the 1970's.

    True   False, the correct word is _____

STRATEGIZE

Complete the check numbers 873 to 875 for each of the scenarios presented on the stub next to each check. You may look at the prior page for details and instructions about how to correctly fill in the information on a check.

Check Stub	Checks To Write

Check Stub

Date
October 7, 2014

Company
Clong Electric

Amount
$64.31

Memo
September
Electric

YMBA Student
4 Success Blvd.
Beautiful, State 98765 USA
info@ymbagroup.com

58-6499/5758   873

Date _____

Pay To The Order Of: _____ $ [   ]

_____ Dollars

America United Bank

memo: _____   Signature: _____
I: 575864996∎:   II∎ 75896998II   0873

Date
October 16, 2014

Company
Ace Tennis Club

Amount
$30.50

Memo
November
Tennis

YMBA Student
4 Success Blvd.
Beautiful, State 98765 USA
info@ymbagroup.com

58-6499/5758   874

Date _____

Pay To The Order Of: _____ $ [   ]

_____ Dollars

America United Bank

memo: _____   Signature: _____
I: 575864996∎:   II∎ 75896998II   0874

Date
October 21, 2014

Company
TSHS Book Store

Amount
$25.82

Memo
History Books

YMBA Student
4 Success Blvd.
Beautiful, State 98765 USA
info@ymbagroup.com

58-6499/5758   875

Date _____

Pay To The Order Of: _____ $ [   ]

_____ Dollars

America United Bank

memo: _____   Signature: _____
I: 575864996∎:   II∎ 75896998II   0875

APPLY

omplete the checks using the information from number 1 and 2 below.
ext, answer question 3 to show the new balance in your check register.

Check 1

YMBA Student
4 Success Blvd.
Beautiful, State 98765 USA
SmartStudent@ymba7.com

58-6499/5758   877

Date _____

Pay To The Order Of: _____ $ [   ]

_____ Dollars

America United Bank

memo: _____   Signature: _____

I: 575864996■:   II■ 7589699 8 II   0876

Check 2

YMBA Student
4 Success Blvd.
Beautiful, State 98765 USA
SmartStudent@ymba7.com

58-6499/5758   878

Date _____

Pay To The Order Of: _____ $ [   ]

_____ Dollars

America United Bank

memo: _____   Signature: _____

I: 575864996■:   II■ 7589699 8 II   0877

1. You attend the dentist, Dr. Gold, and pay with a check the full amount due of $39.00 on November 7, 2014.

2. Your cable television bill to SatTV arrives and you owe $30. You write and mail the check on November 12, 2014.

3. Before you wrote the two checks above your checking account had a balance of $325. What is the new balance in your checking account?

$ [   ]

THINK

Number the items below in the correct order to show the path of a check.

☐ Money Deposits Into The Check Receivers Bank Account. Payment has been made.

☐ Check Writers Bank Withdraws Money From The Check Writers Bank Account

☐ Check Receivers Bank Sends Check Information To A Clearing House

☐ CUSTOMER WRITES CHECK

☐ The Clearing House Sends The Check Information To The Check Writers Bank

☐ Check Receiver Signs The Check Back To Endorse The Check And Deposits Check At A Bank

☐ Check Pays For Goods Or Services

Dear Bank Customer,

Regrettably, it appears that a check you recently wrote was for an amount greater than the amount in your bank account. As a result, the check number 816 for $425.00 was not paid.

The bank has charged your bank checking account $25 for the bounced check due to having insufficient funds to pay the check.

The amount of $25 was deducted from your account this morning. Be sure to note the $25 deduction in your check register.

Sincerely,

Mr. Brown Pants
Your Bank Manager

STRATEGIZE

The Drawing Board

Consider the following purchase scenarios. In the space provided indicate the most likely type of payment. Choose payment types from the tool box below.

TOOL BOX

Trade	ATM Card	Check	Unsecured Loan (family)
Cash	Electronic Payment	Credit Card	Secured Loan (bank)

1. You visit the dentist and pay an $85 invoice.

_____

2. You are going out with friends later and would like to have $20 cash from your bank account.

_____

3. You are planning on going to college and need to pay for the first semester of classes.

_____

4. After school you stop for a slice of pizza.

_____

5. You finished book seven in a series. Your friend has not read book seven, but just finished book 5.

_____

6. Your favorite video game just broke. You would like a new one, but have to wait eight weeks to have enough allowance money to afford a new game.

_____

7. You are on the internet at an on-line store and found a wonderful birthday gift for your mother.

_____

8. Your family just bought a new house.

_____

EXPLORE

The Drawing Board

Interest is the added money to your deposit or investment. The cash in an account is called principal. Interest is generally added monthly, quarterly or annually and added to the principal. Compute the amount of interest earned on the investments below.

Principal x Interest Rate x Time = Interest Earned In That Time

8,000 x .02 x 1 year = $160

Pump Up Interest

1. A savings account has a $500 balance for one year with an interest rate of 2%. How much interest will be added to the account by the bank? $ _____

   $500 x .02 x 1 year = _____

2. A checking account has a $2,000 balance for two years with an interest rate of 1%. How much interest will be added to the account by the bank? $ _____

3. A college savings account has a $4,000 balance for one year with an interest rate of 3%. How much interest will be added to the account by the bank? $ _____

4. In a second savings account you have an $800 balance that earns 3% interest for three years. How much interest will be added to the account by the bank? $ _____

5. How much interest did you earn in total on all investments?

   $ _____

APPLY

The Drawing Board

Who Owns Me?

Listed below are two different company organizational charts. The first company, Razzle Dazzle Toy Company has three divisions. The second company, Sun 2 Sea 2 Snow Travel Inc. has three subsidiaries. Be creative! List three possible ideas for division names in the Razzle Dazzle Toy Company and three ideas that could be subsidiary names for the Sun 2 Sea 2 Snow Travel company.

Division Organizational Chart

Razzle Dazzle Toy Company

Ivy Doll & Friends

1.

2.

Subsidiary Organizational Chart

Sun 2 Sea 2 Snow Travel Inc.

Hot Snow Resorts Co.

3.

4.

A MERGER is when two businesses come together.
An ACQUISITION is when one company buys another business and keeps only some parts of the bought company.

CREATE

Copyright Protected.   45   www.YMBAgroup.com

The Drawing Board

Finance Is Fun

Solve the word search using the words in the tool box below.

TOOL BOX

market	laissez	freedom	jobs	taxes	production
economy	faire	innovate	profit	company	demand

```
n  x  t  a  x  e  s  z  e  f
t  o  v  e  e  k  e  p  t  r
i  f  i  x  k  s  o  k  a  e
f  j  a  t  s  r  c  l  v  e
o  t  o  i  c  m  a  j  o  d
r  i  a  b  r  u  t  m  n  o
p  l  y  k  s  e  d  o  n  m
e  c  o  n  o  m  y  o  i  i
i  y  n  a  p  m  o  c  r  x
d  e  m  a  n  d  b  y  o  p
```

Solve the cryptogram below.

The letters Y M B A and F U N have already been solved.

A	B	C	D	E	F	G	H	I	J	K	L	M	N	O	P	Q	R	S	T	U	V	W	X	Y	Z
19	20				24							25	4							11				8	

$$\underset{17}{}\ \underset{1}{}\ \overset{M}{\underset{25}{}}\ \underset{14}{}\ \underset{21}{}\ \underset{18}{}\ \underset{2}{}\ \underset{1}{}\ \overset{N}{\underset{4}{}}$$

$$\overset{M}{\underset{25}{}}\ \underset{1}{}\ \underset{18}{}\ \underset{2}{}\ \underset{23}{}\ \overset{A}{\underset{19}{}}\ \underset{18}{}\ \underset{21}{}\ \underset{10}{}$$

$$\overset{A}{\underset{19}{}}\qquad \overset{B}{\underset{20}{}}\ \overset{U}{\underset{11}{}}\ \underset{10}{}\ \underset{2}{}\ \overset{N}{\underset{4}{}}\ \underset{21}{}\ \underset{10}{}\ \underset{10}{}$$

$$\underset{18}{}\ \underset{1}{}\qquad \underset{2}{}\ \overset{N}{\underset{4}{}}\ \underset{23}{}\ \underset{21}{}\ \overset{N}{\underset{4}{}}\ \underset{18}{}.$$

STRATEGIZE

TOOL BOX

| Laissez - Faire | Socialism | For Profit Company |
| Communism | Capitalism | Non-Profit Company |

Imagine you were just brushing your teeth and ran out of toothpaste. **Circle one** of the words in the tool box to describe the marketplace where you shop. Next, **create a comic strip** to share a creative, funny story about the trip from your home to the store to purchase a new tube of toothpaste. Be sure to **include details** about your marketplace as you describe your trip to the store.

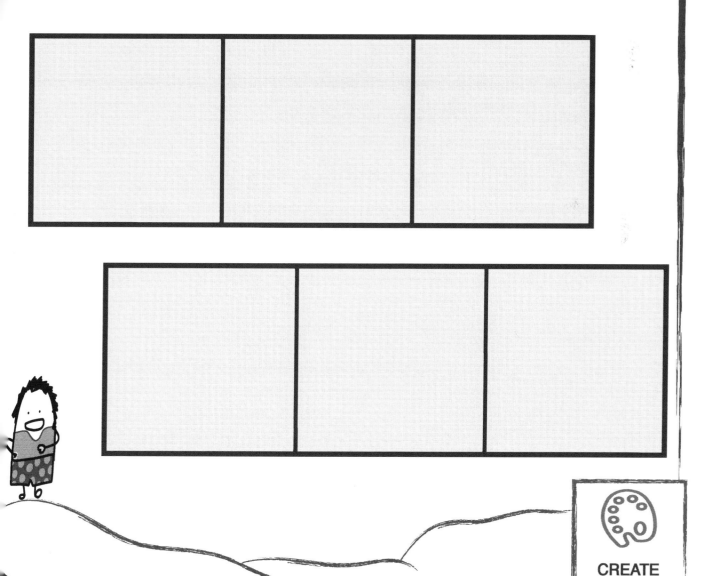

CREATE

The Drawing Board

An incorporated company will likely have a Board of Directors. Imagine the Board of Directors for each of your stock investments voted to approve the payment of common stock dividends. The questions below show the total dollar amount to be shared among the common stock shareholders as a dividend. First compute the dividend to be paid, per share by using division. Next, compute your total dividend amount by multiplying the dividend by your number of shares.

1. P2A Games Incorporated approved a total dividend pay out of $21,000. The company has a total of 14,000 shares outstanding.

Your Common Stock Portfolio

Company	Shares You Own
P2A Games Incorporated	1000 Shares
Sloppy Shirt Company	20 Shares
Health Ye, Health Ye Cereal Co.	100 Shares
Red, White and Glue Corp.	400 Shares
New Snow Each Week Resorts Inc.	50 Shares

Dividend Per Share: $ _____

Total Dividends Paid To Me: $ _____

2. Sloppy Shirt Company approved a total dividend pay out of $12,600. The company has a total of 3,000 shares outstanding.

Dividend Per Share: $ _____   Total Dividends Paid To Me: $ _____

3. Health Ye, Health Ye Cereal Co. approved a total dividend pay out of $30,000. The company has a total of 15,000 shares outstanding.

Dividend Per Share: $ _____   Total Dividends Paid To Me: $ _____

4. Red, white and Glue Corp. approved a total dividend pay out of $16,400. The company has a total of 8,000 shares outstanding.

Dividend Per Share: $ _____   Total Dividends Paid To Me: $ _____

5. New Snow Each Week Resorts Inc. approved a total dividend pay out of $5,250. The company has a total of 3000 shares outstanding.

Dividend Per Share: $ _____   Total Dividends Paid To Me: $ _____

EXPLORE

The Drawing Board

Complete the worksheet below with a friend. First, ask your friend to
select a word for each blank that is in the category shown below the blank.
After all blanks have an answer read the page aloud to your friend.

_____ Incorporated has just competed its red herring to tell
　　　Noun

_____ about the stock the company is going to offer for sale.
Type of animal, plural

_____ your phone alerts you a call is coming in on your phone.
　Funny sound

Your best friend, _____ , invited you to meet at the
　　　　　　　　　Friends name

_____ to read the stock details in the red herring together.
　　Place

When you arrive you are _____ to see the local _____
　　　　　　　　　　　　　Emotion　　　　　　　　　　　　　　　Verb ending in -ing

group _____ on their _____ . Your friend
　　　Verb ending in -ing　　　　　　Body part, plural

arrives and you call out your best friend secret code sound "_____"
　　　　　　　　　　　　　　　　　　　　　　　　　　　　　　　　　　　Funny sound

to get their attention.

As you are both sitting on a _____ reading the red herring
　　　　　　　　　　　　　　　Thing to sit on

many exciting details of future company plans are revealed. For example,

the company will release _____ _____
　　　　　　　　　　　　　　Number　　　　　Small, tiny object, plural

down a steep hill for a contest. The winner will need to successfully

_____ over at least _____ of the objects. The
　Verb, singular　　　　　　　　　　　　Number

contest will repeat until there is a winner.

You and your best friend agree to invest in the stock and say

good-bye with your secret _____ hand shake.
　　　　　　　　　　　　　　　Animal

| A red herring gives details about a new company stock. |

CREATE

The Drawing Board

Bull or Bear?

Stocks overall move up or move down in the stock market.
In a bull market average stock prices are going up.
In a bear market average stock prices are going down.

Examine the average stock prices shown below for the months of June, July, August and September. Circle if the stock prices trending are likely part of a bull or a bear market.

	Jun	Jul	Aug	Sep	Circle One	
1. Stock Price History:	$18.14	$18.60	$19.10	$19.50	Bull	Bear
2. Stock Price History:	$59.00	$63.20	$65.00	$68.12	Bull	Bear
3. Stock Price History:	$17.43	$16.90	$14.10	$12.80	Bull	Bear
4. Stock Price History:	$117.40	$111.46	$104.71	$99.25	Bull	Bear
5. Stock Price History:	$19.00	$22.60	$28.30	$29.40	Bull	Bear
6. Stock Price History:	$15.00	$13.50	$13.40	$11.80	Bull	Bear
7. Stock Price History:	$11.90	$11.10	$10.60	$10.00	Bull	Bear

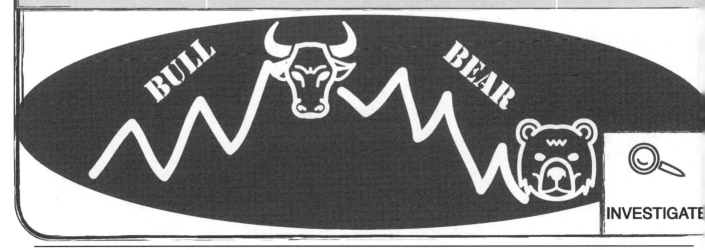

INVESTIGATE

The Drawing Board

Imagine it is your birthday. As a gift you just received a savings bond. Enter a number from the list at the bottom of the page into the square box to explain and identify the parts of the savings bond.

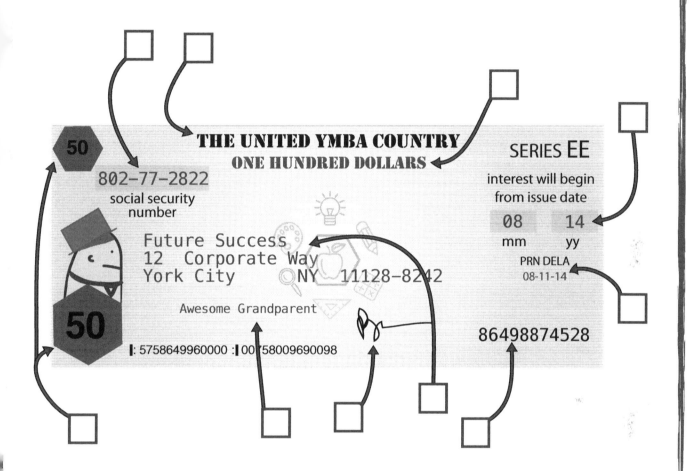

1. The maturity value of the savings bond.

2. The signature or name of a company representative that issued the bond.

3. The government that issued the savings bond and will be paying interest to the owner.

4. Social Security Number of person who will own the savings bond.

5. Since the savings bond owner is under 18 years old a parent or guardian.

6. The name and street address of the owner of the savings bond.

7. The date the savings bond was printed.

8. The value of the savings bond spelt out in words.

9. The month and year when the savings bond interest earnings begin.

10. The bond serial number. This number is unique to each savings bond.

APPLY

The Drawing Board

Imagine each savings bond had a family of its own. Using the bond types shown in the tool box below match the family vacation details that would best describe the family of that type of savings bond.

1. My family - When my family and I go on vacation we like to try a different adventure each day. We let our friends and family know that we have no plans from one time to the next. That each day will be something new. They just never know what pictures we will share next! If my family and I were a savings bond we would be a _____ bond.

2. My family - When my family and I go on vacation we stay very active. We like to skydive over mountains, roller blade with one skate and pet exotic animals that have very big teeth. We are new to traveling, but we enjoy driving without a map and following to road. Sometimes we try to find the hotel without a map or directions. (A few nights we ended up camping rather than staying at a hotel). If my family and I were a savings bond we would be a _____ bond.

3. My family - When my family and I go on vacation we enjoy taking a few years to plan the trip. We do not travel while we wait for the vacation to arrive. But, we have fun talking about the trip and making plans for when trip date arrives. If my family and I were a savings bond we would be a _____ bond.

4. My family - When my family and I go on vacation we make a deal that if we each do not have a wonderful vacation that we will plan a new vacation when we get back home. The back up vacation plan helps each of us have a bit less worry about each detail of the vacation. If one vacation is not an awesome adventure then we always have a back up plan! If my family and I were a savings bond we would be a _____ bond.

BOND TYPES   TOOL BOX

| Zero Coupon Bond | Floating Rate Bond |
| Junk Bond | Asset Backed Bond |

EXPLORE

Would you select an aggressive strategy with high risk investments?
Do you prefer a conservative investment strategy with a low risk of loss?
Perhaps you prefer a combination of high risk and low risk investments?

As you read each item below circle a choice in the column to indicate what you would likely choose. "Yes" if you would make the same decision, "Maybe" if you would consider the item and "No" if would not make the same decision.

1. I would invest in a mutual fund that has a high risk of not being profitable, but if profitable would double my investment.	No	Maybe	Yes
2. I would purchase stock in a new company.	No	Maybe	Yes
3. I would loan money without having a written agreement signed by the person receiving the money.	No	Maybe	Yes
4. I would purchase 100 shares of stock in a company at a price of $11.85 a share that I did not research.	No	Maybe	Yes
5. I would open a savings account at a new bank in town.	No	Maybe	Yes
6. I would buy a car on the internet without having time to see or inspect the car before paying.	No	Maybe	Yes
7. I would pay $5 to play a bingo game with a $1,000 prize.	No	Maybe	Yes
8. I would mail a credit card payment three days before the date the payment is due to be received by the company.	No	Maybe	Yes

Low Risk = 8 – 14 points
Medium Risk = 15 – 19 points
High Risk = 20 – 24 points

What is your investment style?

For each "Yes" add 3 points.
For each "Maybe" add 2 points.
For each "No" add 1 point.

INVESTIGATE

Compute the balance for the following investment descriptions:

1. Clara receives an account statement in the mail. The statement shows the total amount she deposited as $2,640. It also shows the interest earned is 5%. What is total balance of her 529 college savings account?

$2,640 x .05 = $132

Amount Deposited: $2,640.
Interest Earned: + $132.
The total account balance is $2,772.

2. Ella has been investing all her childcare money in a 529 college savings account. She has a total balance of $850 with 4% interest earned on the $850. What is total balance of her 529 college savings account?

3. Cody has a 401k retirement account at his job. He has been investing $100 a month into his account. His employer has a 100% match to the employee contributions. After one year what is the total balance deposited into his account?

4. Ken has been adding $40 a month to the 529 college savings account of his brother Sven for the past 6 months. Sven receives his investment statement and notices the $500 he deposited, but also notices the balance shows an additional deposit. What is the total amount his account increased over the past 6 months?

5. Ruby has a 529 savings account with a balance of $6,000. She also has a 401k retirement account with a balance of $2,400. Both accounts are expected to earn 4% interest next year. If all goes as planned, what will be the balance in each account? What is the total balance of both accounts?

COMPUTE

Congratulations! You have become a wise investor and have been successful at saving some of your money. Find the solution to the three problems below. Add the three totals together to learn the total balance of your investments.

(see the example at the bottom of the prior page for a hint)

1. On January 1 of last year your savings account had a $200 balance. Your account earned 2% during the year. What is your savings account balance on December 31 of the same year?

2. On January 1 of last year you began a financial plan to invest $25 a month into your 529 college savings account. The account earned 5% interest for the year. What is your savings account balance on December 31 of the same year?

3. During the last year your family offered to pay you $2 a week for each week the chores were completed at the house. There are 52 weeks in a year. Two weeks you did not do chores. One week you were out of town so chores were not done during that week as well. You spent half of the chore money during the year. The other half you saved in a safe in your bedroom. What was the total amount of chore money you had as of December 31 last year?

4. How much do you in total investments at the end of the year?

$ _____ + $ _____ + $ _____ = $ _____

The formula to know an amount of interest is:

Interest = Principal x Rate x Time

COMPUTE

The Drawing Board

A service that a bank offers a customer is a money loan. When a customer decides to request a loan they will complete an application. The bank will review the application and examine the application details regarding the candidates work experience and credit report history. A final decision will be made as either "approved" or "denied". Approved indicates the person will receive the money from the bank. Denied indicates that the bank was not able to approve the loan and the customer will not receive the money.

For the scenarios below imagine you are the loan manager at Buck City Bank. Circle your loan decision next to each scenario as either approved or denied.

1. This credit report is better than __82__ % when compared to other credit reports.
   The length of employment has been __11__ years at the same job.
   The applicant will work __2__ days each month to earn the money to pay the loan.
   The applicant has used __10__ % of the credit limit available on their credit cards.

   APPROVED   **DENIED**

2. This credit report is better than __30__ % when compared to other credit reports.
   The length of employment has been __4__ years at the same job.
   The applicant will work __7__ days each month to earn the money to pay the loan.
   The applicant has used __75__ % of the credit limit available on their credit cards.

   APPROVED   **DENIED**

3. This credit report is better than __90__ % when compared to other credit reports.
   The length of employment has been __16__ years at the same job.
   The applicant will work __1__ day each month to earn the money to pay the loan.
   The applicant has used __12__ % of the credit limit available on their credit cards.

   APPROVED   **DENIED**

4. This credit report is better than __45__ % when compared to other credit reports.
   The length of employment has been __1__ year at the same job.
   The applicant will work __8__ days each month to earn the money to pay the loan.
   The applicant has used __80__ % of the credit limit available on their credit cards.

   APPROVED   **DENIED**

STRATEGIZE

Basic math skills are needed in every business and even when making personal shopping or investment decisions. In the business world common questions include: What is the cost of purchasing these supplies? How should I price the product? How profitable is the company? Personal finance questions may include: How much interest does my savings account earn? How much interest am I paying on my car loan? How much should I save for college?

Consider numbers as having their own personal style. At times the data being studied may be a percentage, such as 75%. At other times the data may be a fraction, shown as $\frac{3}{4}$. A different piece of data may be .75, a decimal. Each of the three shown in this paragraph are equal to three-quarters of the whole.

FRACTION

A corporation stock price has a value of $34\frac{3}{4}$.

PERCENT

The shipping box inventory has 50% remaining in stock.

DECIMAL

The sales employees each worked 38.5 hours last week.

Fill in the blanks below to show each number as an equivalent fraction, decimal and percent.

	Fraction	Decimal	Percent
1.	$\frac{1}{2}$	☐	☐
2.	☐	.25	☐
3.	$\frac{4}{10}$	☐	☐
4.	☐	☐	75%
5.	☐	.8	☐

Percent To Fraction:	*Decimal To Percent:*	*Decimal To Fraction:*	
A Percent Is A Part Of 100.	.25 = 2 5 = 25%	.25 = $\frac{25}{100}$	**COMPUTE**
$\frac{54}{100}$ = 54% *Mean 54 Parts of the 100 Total Parts*	Move the decimal point two places right and add the "%" sign for a percent.	A decimal is part of a whole. Example: .99 + .01 = 1 whole = $\frac{100}{100}$	

www.YMBAgroup.com

Review the question and answer shown for number one below. Next, complete questions two and three to compute the time until the balance is paid to $0.

1. A credit card has a balance of $2,000. Interest added to the account is $20 a month. How many months until the balance is paid off if paying $100 a month?

$2,000 balance divided by $100 a month payment = 20 months to pay charges.
There is also $20 a month interest for each of the 20 months.
$20 x 20 months to pay off balance = $400.
How many months would it be to pay the $400 in interest costs?
$400 interest charged divided by $100 a month payment = 4 months.
Total time to pay off the credit card = 24 months.
In ___2___ years and ___0___ months the balance will be paid. $ $ $

2. A credit card has a balance of $500. Interest added to the account is $20 a month. How many months until the balance is paid off if paying $100 a month?

$_____ balance divided by $____ a month payment = ____ months to pay charges.
There is also $_____ a month interest for each of the _____ months.
Monthly interest $_____X_____ months to pay balance = $_____ interest charged
How many months would it be to pay the $_____ in interest costs?
$_____ interest charged divided by $_____ a month payment = _____ months.
Total time to pay off the credit card charges and interest costs = _____ months.
In _____ years and _____ months the balance will be paid. $ $ $

3. A credit card has a balance of $3,000. Interest added to the account is $10 a month. How many months until the balance is paid off if paying $50 a month?

$_____ balance divided by $____ a month payment = ____ months to pay charges.
There is also $_____ a month interest for each of the _____ months.
Monthly interest $_____X_____ months to pay balance = $_____ interest charged
How many months would it be to pay the $_____ in interest costs?
$_____ interest charged divided by $_____ a month payment = _____ months.
Total time to pay off the credit card charges and interest costs = _____ months.
In _____ years and _____ months the balance will be paid.

$ $ $

APPLY

Imagine you are preparing to purchase your first home. You know the importance of having an accurate credit report. You request a copy of your most recent credit report to confirm it is correct. Answer the questions below. If the credit report shows the correct information simply mark the item as correct. If the item is not correct mark it as incorrect and write the correct information.

1. In January of 2014 Credit Agency 2 reported your payment as late.

    Correct   Not Correct _____

2. The credit limit on your First Choice Master Card is $4,000.

    Correct   Not Correct _____

3. The credit card number for your First Choice Master Card ends in 6724.

    Correct   Not Correct _____

4. The First Choice Master Card was opened in 2005.

    Correct   Not Correct _____

5. The First Choice Master Card company is located in Dallas, Texas.

    Correct   Not Correct _____

... Sample Credit Report Section ...

First Choice Master Card		Credit Agency 1	Credit Agency 2	Credit Agency 3
+ Positive Account	Account Name	First Choice Master Card	First Choice MC	First Choice MasterCa
	Account #	11251XXXX	11251XXXX	1125XXXXXXXX4424
	Account Type	Revolving Credit Card	Credit Card	Credit Card
	Balance	$174.00	$178.00	$178.00
PO BOX 162244	Past Due			
WARREN, MI 48090	Date Opened	6/1/2009	6/1/2009	6/2009
	Account Status	Open	Open	Open
	Mo. Payment			
	Payment Status	Pays on time.	Account in good standing.	Account in good standing.
	High Balance	$483.00	$483.00	$483.00
	Limit	$2,000.00		$2,000.00
	Terms			
	Comments		Pays on time.	Pays on time.

History of Payments/24 Months

Month	2012						2013												2014		
	JUL	AUG	SEP	OCT	NOV	DEC	JAN	FEB	MAR	APR	MAY	JUN	JUL	AUG	SEP	OCT	NOV	DEC	JAN	FEB	MAR
agency 1	OK	OK	OK	OK	OK	OK	OK	OK	OK	OK	OK	OK	OK	OK	OK	OK	OK	OK	OK	OK	OK
agency 2	OK	OK	OK	OK	OK	OK	OK	OK	OK	OK	OK	OK	OK	OK	OK	OK	OK	OK	OK	OK	OK
agency 3	OK	OK	OK	OK	OK	OK	OK	OK	OK	OK	OK	OK	OK	OK	OK	OK	OK	OK	OK	OK	OK

INVESTIGATE

Total Monthly Paymen

Consider the following financial questions below. Write your answers in the space provided. Be sure to write the formula used to solve each question.

1. A department store invoice shows the following charges: 1 pair of sneakers $74.95, 1 designer watch by $95.00, 2 pairs of jeans at $50 each. What is the total amount of the invoice?

2. The stock value for Floopy-Doopy Toy Company is $34.25 per share. You have 12 shares of stock. What is the total value of your stock?

3. You are preparing a deposit to bring to the bank for your job at Fluffy Pet Shop. The four checks are written for the following amounts: $20, $41.75, $108.40, $18.12 What is the total amount you of your deposit to write on the bank deposit slip?

4. In 2012 your savings account earned $5.25 interest. In 2013 your savings account earned $5.40 interest. In 2014 your account interest total is $5.50. What is the total amount of interest earned?

5. You invested $30 a month for the past 11 months to a 529 college savings account. What was the total amount you invested in your college savings account?

6. The Silly Top Circus is coming to town in five months. A ticket to the show is $50. How much do you need to save each month to purchase a ticket for both you and your best friend to see the show?

THINK

A Piece of Pie

Consider the investment strategy pie charts below. Label each pie chart piece as indicated by writing the percent in the square box provided.

1.

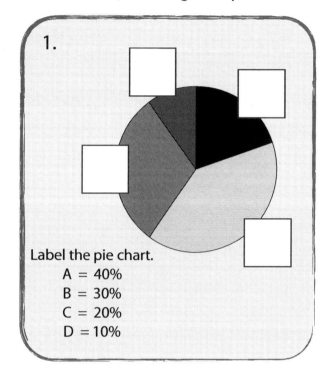

Label the pie chart.
- A = 40%
- B = 30%
- C = 20%
- D = 10%

2.   Label the pie chart.
Conservative, low risk = 75%
Aggressive, high risk = 25%

3.   What is the dollar value of each section?
- A = 25%
- B = 25%
- C = 50%

The pie chart shows the diversification mix with an investment total value of $12,000.

4.   An investor has 50% invested in moderate risk stocks. 35% invested in conservative, low-risk stocks and 15% invested in high risk stock.
Label the pie chart to accurately show the pie sections as high, moderate, low.

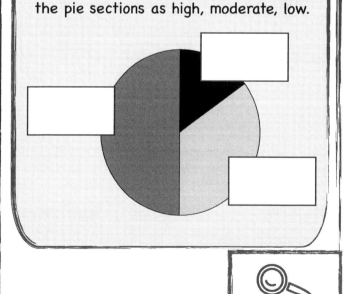

INVESTIGATE

www.YMBAgroup.com

The Drawing Board

Congratulations! You have just been promoted to the position of financial advisor at Kash and Pyle Savings Bank.

Today you have appointments with six different bank customers who are seeking your suggestions on a custom investment strateg

Match the bank customer in column one to the investment strategy you would suggest to best match the age, risk level and financial goals of the customer.

Investment Risk Strategy

TOOL BOX

(A) Low Risk   (B) Medium to High Risk   (C) Low to Medium Risk

(D) Medium Risk   (E) High Risk   (F) No Risk to Low Risk

(1) _____ Customer 1 just had their 18th birthday.

(2) _____ Customer 2 is a college student.

(3) _____ Customer 3 just began their first job.

(4) _____ Customer 4 is buying their first house today.

(5) _____ Customer 5 just celebrated 15 years at a job.

(6) _____ Customer 6 is enjoying their retirement.

(7) If you were to invest $100 today which investment risk strategy would you select and why? _____

_____

THINK

ACCOUNTING

Economics & Budgeting

Imagine you are the inventory control manager at RubbAir Tire Company. Review the accounting data below and calculate the result.

1. The company spent $3,045 on tires in December to purchase a total of 145 tire How much did one tire cost the company?

    The cost per tire was: $ _____

2. The company sold 145 tires to customers in December. The sale price per tire was $85 each. What is the total sales revenue (how much customers paid)?

    The total sales revenue was: $ _____

3. The state requires the company to charge 7% sales tax to customers on their purchases. How much sales tax was collected with the sale of 145 tires?

    The total state sales tax collected was: $ _____

4. The profit the company earned by selling 145 tires is equal to the total tire sales less the cost of purchasing the tires from the tire supplier.
    What is the profit for these tires?
    The profit from selling the 145 tires is: $ _____

5. A supplier has just informed the company that the price of tires has increased to $25 per tire. How much will the company spend to purchase the same number of tires next year?
    The cost of purchasing 145 tires next year will be: $ _____

COMPUTE

The Drawing Board

Would You Rather...

Circle the asset below that is a greater dollar value to the company.

1. (a) Checking account, value $3,000   (b) Savings account, value $4,000

2. (a) Office copier, value $900   (b) Office printer, value $400

3. (a) Office supplies, value $300   (b) Cleaning supplies, value $150

4. (a) Inventory, 10 cases at $120 each   (b) Inventory, 21 cases at $85 each

5. (a) 18 Stock shares at $4.35 each   (b) 32 Stock shares at $2.50 each

6. (a) 4 Trucks, value $9,200 each   (b) 6 Cars, value $7,800 each

7. (a) 12 Uniforms, value $42 each   (b) 35 Promotional t-shirts, value $8 each

8. (a) 4 Computers, value $930 each   (b) 7 Televisions, value $345 each

9. (a) 3,200 Labels, value .20 each   (b) 210 Shipping boxes, value $1.85 each

10. (a) 9 Desks, value $125 each   (b) 45 Chairs, value $95 each

CURRENT ASSET is cash, or can be sold for cash, within one year or less.

NON-CURRENT ASSET any item of value that will take one year or more to sell.

STRATEGIZE

The Drawing Board

Reducing With LIFO

Consider the recent sales at Sports Den. Find the total dollar amount the inventory will be reduced using the LIFO method.

1. 16 volleyballs were sold in the month of September.

    Retail cost per volleyball: $14.00

    75 volleyball's purchased for inventory in August, 2013: $6.00

    Inventory cost per volleyball purchased August, 2012: $5.00

    Inventory reduction value using LIFO: $ _____

2. 52 pairs of Zip running sneakers were sold in the month of August.

    Retail cost per pair of Zip running sneakers: $30.00

    85 sneakers purchased for inventory in May, 2013: $12.00

    Inventory cost per pair of sneakers purchased August, 2012: $9.00

    Inventory reduction value using LIFO: $ _____

3. 214 baseballs were sold in the month of August.

    Retail cost per baseball: $4.00

    300 baseball's purchased for inventory in September, 2013: $2.50

    Inventory cost per baseball purchased March, 2012: $2.00

    Inventory reduction value using LIFO: $ _____

4. 25 4-person tents were sold in the month of August.

    Retail cost per 4-person tent: $89.00

    40 4-person tent's purchased for inventory in June, 2013: $50.00

    Inventory cost per 4-person tent purchased April, 2012: $47.00

    Inventory reduction value using LIFO: $ _____

COMPUTE

---

 www.YMBAgroup.com

The Drawing Board

Match the term with the word it is describing.
Draw a line to match the term to the definition.

current asset

An amount a company owes, a debt to pay.

LIFO

The inventory method that values sold inventory based on the first purchased cost.

liability

An item owned by a company that is cash or can be sold for cash in one year or less.

FIFO

A place to group similar revenues, expenses, assets or liabilities in accounting.

account

The inventory method that values sold inventory based on the last purchased cost.

non-current asset

An item owned by a company that is cash or can be sold for cash in more than one year.

tangible asset

A non-physical item that adds value to a company operations.

inventory

Goods held by a company that are offered for sale to customers.

intangible asset

A physical item that has a money value.

EXPLORE

www.YMBAgroup.com

The Drawing Board

Three invoices for ColorTube Printers Corp. are shown below. The stamp on each shows the date the invoice was paid. Enter the amount that should have been paid based on the date the invoice was actually paid in the area provided.

Examine each invoice for the terms and late fees, if any, to add to the balance due.

National Paper Supply House, Inc.

INVOICE NUMBER: 8752

December 7, 2014

DUE DATE: DECEMBER 21, 2014, NET 15

Quantity	Stock Number	Item Details	Each	Total Price
12	472G			$180.00
10	657R		$9	$99.00

PAID DECEMBER 28, 2014

Sub-Total	$279.00
State Sales Tax 7%	$19.53
Total	$298.53

IF PAID BEYOND NET 10 ADD $25 LATE FEE.

1. Payment Amount

$ _____

Better Brown Box Business Company

INVOICE NUMBER: 1074

December 12, 2014

DUE DATE: NET 30 FROM INVOICE DATE

Quantity	Stock Number	Item Details	h	Total Price
100	FB4	Standar		$470.00
100	FQ5			$310.00

PAID DECEMBER 28, 2014

Sub-Total	$780.00
State Sales Tax 6%	$46.80
Total	$826.80

2. Payment Amount

$ _____

Rush Flash Delivery Service   Monthly Statement

INVOICE NUMBER: D435

December 18, 2014

DUE DATE: DUE ON RECEIPT OF INVOICE. AFTER 10 DAYS ADD 10% LATE FEE.

Quantity	Stock Number	Item Details	Total Price
24	32h7	Same day	$96.00
18	58m9		$360.00

PAID DECEMBER 30, 2014

Sub-Total	$456.00
State Sales Tax 8%	$36.48
Total	$492.48

3. Payment Amount

$ _____

APPLY

The Drawing Board

Pay or Receive?

In each of the boxes below is a transaction involving Royal Films Movie Theater. Draw a line from each box to either the accounts payable oval, or the accounts receivable oval, to indicate if the transaction is a receivable or a payable for the movie theater. Remember, if the company purchased the item and owes the money, the amount due will be shown in the *accounts payable* account. If the movie theater sold the item and is waiting to receive payment, the amount is recorded in the *accounts receivable* account.

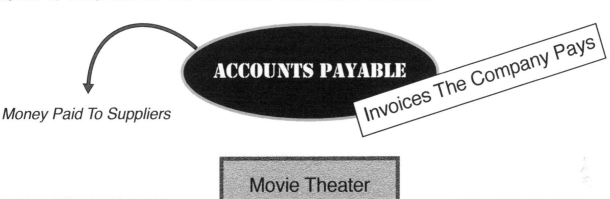

ACCOUNTS PAYABLE

Invoices The Company Pays

Money Paid To Suppliers

Movie Theater Advertising Local Town Billboards

Movie Poster Lobby Display Picture Frame Replacements

Monthly Electric Company Utility Invoice

Party Room Rental Contract Payment Due

Movie Preview Audience Advertising Commercials

Private Movie Screening Contract Payment Due

Money Paid By Customers

Amounts The Company Collects

ACCOUNTS RECEIVABLE

EXPLORE

The Drawing Board

Your job today is to be an accounting superhero. Fill in the missing number to help each company complete their balance sheet. For each of the open spaces enter the amount needed to balance the accounts.

ASSETS = LIABILITIES + OWNERS EQUITY

1. Balance Sheet
1/1/2014 - 12/31/2014

Assets:

Cash	10,000
Accounts Receivable	500
Inventory	3,000
Vehicles	6,000

Liabilities:

Accounts Payable	1,000
Mortgage Payable	2,500
Car Loan:	
Owners Equity:	7,000

2. Balance Sheet
1/1/2014 - 12/31/2014

Assets:

Cash	21,000
Checking Account	4,800
Savings Account	4,200
Accounts Receivable:	7,300
Computers	4,200
Inventory	6,000
Equipment	3,500
Vehicles	9,000

Liabilities:

Accounts Payable	1,000
Mortgage Payable	5,800
Car Loan	3,000
Owners Equity:	

3. Balance Sheet
1/1/2014 - 12/31/2014

Assets:

Cash	
Checking Account	11,800
Savings Account	7,200
Accounts Receivable	7,300
Computers	4,400
Inventory	8,000
Equipment	3,500
Vehicles	2,000

Liabilities:

Accounts Payable	1,000
Mortgage Payable	5,800
Car Loan	3,000
Owners Equity:	28,000

4. Balance Sheet
1/1/2014 - 12/31/2014

Assets:

Cash	12,000
Accounts Receivable	800
Inventory:	3,200
Vehicles	7,000

Liabilities:

Accounts Payable	2,400
Mortgage Payable	3,200
Car Loan	5,000
Owners Equity:	

STRATEGIZE

The Drawing Board

Complete the balance sheet by entering an amount next to each account using the clues provided at the bottom of the page. After all clues are in place use addition and subtraction to enter the amounts for the remaining accounts.

Assets = Liabilities + Equity

Splashy Swimming Pools
Balance Sheet
January 1, 2014 – December 31, 2014

Assets		Liabilities	
Current Assets		**Current Liabilities**	
Cash	$33,000	Accounts Payable	$7,200
Accounts Receivable	(1)	Loan Payments Due	(10)
(less doubtful accounts)	(2)	Taxes Payable	(11)
Inventory	(3)	Total Current Liabilities	$14,000
Prepaid Expenses	$800		
Total Current Assets	(4)	**Long-Term Liabilities**	
		Mortgage	$45,000
Fixed Assets		Equipment Loan	$15,800
Land	(5)	Total Long Term Liabilities	(12)
Building	(6)		
Equipment	(7)	Total Liabilities	(13)
Furniture	$4,000		
Total Fixed Assets	(8)	Owners Equity	$97,800
Total Assets	(9)	Liabilities + Equity	$172,600

1. Splashy Swimming Pools is owed $2,000 from customers, but have listed $200 of the amount as not likely to be paid.

2. Splashy purchased $800 in inventory to be added to the existing inventory balance of $5,200.

3. Total assets for Splashy are $182,000 including the building for $75,000 and the land it is on for $30,600.

4. Equipment has the same value as last year, $21,000.

5. The company just received a $4,000 tax bill.

THINK

Copyright Protected.   71   www.YMBAgroup.com

The Drawing Board

Choosing the most useful combination of financial statements to examine will help make an effective decision. For the questions below choose the more useful group of financial statements.

1. The company is planning on purchasing inventory for the Thanksgiving Holiday Bonanza. The manager should review:

    (a) the last 24 years of statements   (b) the last 3 years of statements

2. The company is considering payroll increases and would like to know how much the payroll has increased since the company opened in 2007.

    (a) all Balance Sheets available   (b) last years Balance Sheet

3. Two years ago the company bought a new fuel efficient car to help reduce the fuel expense for the business. The manager would like to see if there has been a savings in fuel costs.

    (a) the last 8 months of statements   (b) the last 4 years of statements.

4. The company received the annual tax bill and would like to compare it to last years tax expense.

    (a) last years Balance Sheet   (b) last quarters Balance Sheet

5. The owner believes the new furniture bought last month was $1,000. Where can the owner see the sales results from last month?

    (a) last months Balance Sheet   (b) last years Balance Sheet

6. The accountant has requested the total assets for each of the past 5 years. What financial report would be most helpful?

    (a) 5 years of Balance Sheets   (b) 5 quarters of Balance Sheets

BONUS:

    7. What month is the first month in the first quarter of a fiscal year?

    _____

    8. What are the months in the 2nd quarter?

    _____

INVESTIGATE

The Drawing Board

Hooray! You just received your file confirmation in the mail from the Secretary of State for your state. Your corporation is officially registered!

1. Circle your new company industry from the choices in tool box one below.

TOOL BOX ONE

Dentist	Bakery	Ski Instructor	Lawn Service
Photographer	Dog Walker	Book Store	Shoe Store

2. Next, consider the purchases your company will buy to meet the needs of your customers. Circle four expense accounts that your company will use to record the transactions for those purchases.

TOOL BOX TWO

Utilities	Office Supplies	Inventory	Rent or Mortgage
Insurance	Uniforms	Equipment	Educational Training

3. List the four expense categories circled in Tool Box 2. Next, list two possible purchases that may be recorded in each account.

Expense 1: _____   Expense 2: _____

purchase: _____   purchase: _____

purchase: _____   purchase: _____

Expense 3: _____   Expense 4: _____

purchase: _____   purchase: _____

purchase: _____   purchase: _____

CREATE

The Drawing Board

Attention: Bookkeeper, Accounts Payable Clerk and Budget Manager

Date: December 12, 2014

From: Operations Manager

Re: Company increasing service area to three new zip codes

Have a BoInG Day.

As discussed at our meeting the owners of BoInG Bounce Houses have voted to approve a customer service area expansion. The company will seek customers in three new zip codes. This will bring the service area to a total of four zip codes.

The population and income of the three new zip codes is same as the current zip code. There is a very small amount of competition. For these reasons the marketing team has stated they expect the same amount of customer demand. To stay a top company we will offer the super-bounce, mega-water features. Remember to include the Bouncin' Bubbles in the price history.

We ask your departments for a summary of the bounce house purchases over the last three years. This will allow the owners to make reliable decisions about how many new bounce houses to purchase. Also, a second report is requested. The owners need to hire employees to set up and take down the bounce house rentals. How many hours the four employees currently perform bounce house installs and returns each month?

The information is requested by email prior to December 20, 2014.

Read the internal office memo above. An internal memo is sent inside a company and can be sent by email or printed on a piece of paper. Next, answer the following:

1. Why do you think the company needs to buy bounce houses?

2. How can the current inventory number help the owners plan the purchase?

3. What would be the math formula to help the owners compute the number of employees to hire for the new zip code installs and returns?

X _____ **=** _____

_____   _____   _____

THINK

The Drawing Board

Examine the Chart of Accounts on the prior page to answer the questions below. First, in section (A), circle the two accounts changed by the transaction. Next, in section (B), circle to select if the transaction will cause the checking account to "increase", "decrease", or if the transaction will cause "no change". *Reminder, one account will increase and one will decrease with each purchase.*

1. Hula Trio Corp. uses a loan to buy a new hula-hoop bending machine.

   (A)

Account Name	Type	Account Name	Type
Checking	Asset	Accounts Payable	Liability
Accounts Receivable	Asset	Credit Card	Liability
Office Supplies	Asset	Bank Loan	Liability
Machinery	Asset	Taxes Payable	Liability
Equipment	Asset	Retained Earnings	Owners Equity

   (B)   (a) increase   (b) decrease   (c) no change

2. The accountant at the Hula Trio Corp. pays $700 on a credit card.

   (A)

Account Name	Type	Account Name	Type
Checking	Asset	Accounts Payable	Liability
Accounts Receivable	Asset	Credit Card	Liability
Office Supplies	Asset	Bank Loan	Liability
Machinery	Asset	Taxes Payable	Liability
Equipment	Asset	Retained Earnings	Owners Equity

   (B)   (a) increase   (b) decrease   (c) no change

3. The Hula Trio Corp. deposits a check payment from Tunzafun for $315.

   (A)

Account Name	Type	Account Name	Type
Checking	Asset	Accounts Payable	Liability
Accounts Receivable	Asset	Credit Card	Liability
Office Supplies	Asset	Bank Loan	Liability
Machinery	Asset	Taxes Payable	Liability
Equipment	Asset	Retained Earnings	Owners Equity

   (B)   (a) increase   (b) decrease   (c) no change

APPLY

The Drawing Board

Review the income statement for Pete Zah's Pizza Place and answer the questions below. The end of year 2014 results are shown, along with a column to compare the end of the year results with 2013.

PETE ZAH'S PIZZA PLACE
Income Statement
Ending December 31, 2014

	2014	2013
Revenue		
Sales	$278,000	$268,000
Less: Coupons and Returns	$ 11,000	$ 1,000
Total Revenue	$267,000	$267,000
Expenses		
Operating Expense	$147,000	$143,000
Production Expense	$ 82,000	$ 78,000
Interest Expense	$ 3,000	$ 3,000
Net Income Before Taxes	$232,000	$224,000
Taxes	$ 12,000	$ 11,000
Total Expenses	$244,000	$235,000
Net Income	$ 23,000	$ 32,000

Did you know ...
Two lines show the final total on a financial statement. (One line shows a sub-total.)

1. Did the sales amount increase or decrease from 2013 – 2014? _____

2. What are the net sales at the end of 2013? _____ and ending 2014? _____

3. If the sales total changed from 2013 to 2014 how is the total revenue number the same?

4. What is a possible reason why production costs increased from 2013 to 2014?

5. How is it possible to have less sales, but a higher profit, one year to the next?

6. The company expects sales growth to stay the same. What is an approximate expected sales amount for the end of 2015? _____

THINK

The Drawing Board

Let's Dance!

Dance Pals!, a dance school for children, is reviewing three years of business results. Complete the questions below to help the company analyze the results in the five accounts below.

	2012	2013	2014
Rent Paid	$12,000	$14,200	$15,400
Sales	$78,000	$84,000	$90,000
Payroll	$40,000	$45,000	$45,000
Car Loans	$ 4,000	$22,000	$20,000
Sales Tax Paid	$ 7,800	$ 8,400	$ 9,000

1. Did the company sales from 2012 to 2014 increase, decrease or stay the same?

      increase   decrease   stay the same

2. What is the amount of the sales change from 2012 to 2014? $_____.

3. What is the amount of the payroll change from 2012 to 2014? $_____.

4. In which year did the company buy a new car with a car loan? $_____.

5. What is the cost of the rent, per month, in 2013? $_____.

6. If the 2 employees at Dance Pals! are paid equally how much did each employee receive as payroll in 2012? $_____.

7. BONUS:

   What is the sales tax rate in 2014? (a percent of sales) _____%

EXPLORE

The Drawing Board

Consider the four ratio examples below. Compare the results with the lesson on the prior page. What do the ratio results reveal about the given company?

1. Fresh Farm Snacks has $23,000 in liabilities and $15,000 in equity. The formula to compute the debt to equity ratio is: What does the debt to equity ratio answer of 1.53 reveal about the company debt?

$$\frac{\$23,000}{\$15,000} = 1.53$$

2. Maze Florist has $12,000 in current assets and $5,000 in current liabilities. The formula to compute the current ratio is: What does the ratio answer of 2.4 reveal about how likely a company is to pay its bills?

$$\frac{\$12,000}{\$5,000} = 2.4$$

3. Holden Horse Training has $6,000 in cash and $2,000 in accounts receivable. The formula to compute the quick ratio is: What does the quick ratio answer of 1.6 reveal about how much cash is available to pay bills?

$$\frac{\$6,000 + \$2,000}{\$5,000} = 1.6$$

4. MGL Inc. has a stock price of $7.45 a share and an earnings per share of $2. The formula to compute the price earnings ratio is: What does the ratio answer of 4.23 reveal about the company?

$$\frac{\$7.45}{\$2.00} = 4.23$$

EXPLORE

The Drawing Board

Castle Construction Company, known as C3, just held a Board of Directors meeting. At the meeting decisions were made about how to spend the company profit. A vote was held and the Board decided to spend some of the company earnings profit on dividends to shareholders and a portion of the earnings will be invested in business assets.

Use the data below to compute how the Board of Directors at C3 voted to spend the company profit.

Total Number Of Stock Shares Outstanding: 7,934
Total Company Earnings: $ 295,000
Earnings Per Share (EPS): $10.50
Current Stock Market Share Price: $50.00

- The company voted to replace three windows on the building at a cost of $7,000 total. The company also voted to replace the roof for $12,000.

- The company voted to purchase 1 enclosed trailer and 1 forklift at a total cost of $12,400 each.

- The company voted to purchase 3 new trucks at a total cost of $18,800 each.

- The company voted to give stockholders a dividend payment equal to 25% of earnings.

1. How much (in dollars) did the Board of Directors at C3 approve to distribute (give) stockholders in dividend payments?

2. What is the total dollar amount approved as either a purchase or a dividend payment?

3. Compute the P/E Ratio. What does the result tell an investor about the company?

Another C3 Fantasy Castle

C3

COMPUTE

The Drawing Board

Listed for each question below are the details needed to compute a ratio. What does the ratio tell the manager or owner about the business operations?

1. Stock Market Share Price: $28.00. Earnings per share: $7.

The P/E Ratio is _____. This result informs the manager or owner:

_____

_____

2. Total Liabilities: $44,000. Total Equity: 88,000.

The D/E Ratio is _____. This result informs the manager or owner:

_____

_____

_____

3. Cash Balance: $84,000. Receivables: $4,300. Current Liabilities: $7,700.

The Quick Ratio is _____. This result informs the manager or owner:

_____

_____

_____

4. Current Assets: $250,000. Current Liabilities: $55,250.

The Current Ratio is _____. This result informs the manager or owner:

_____

_____

STRATEGIZE

The Drawing Board

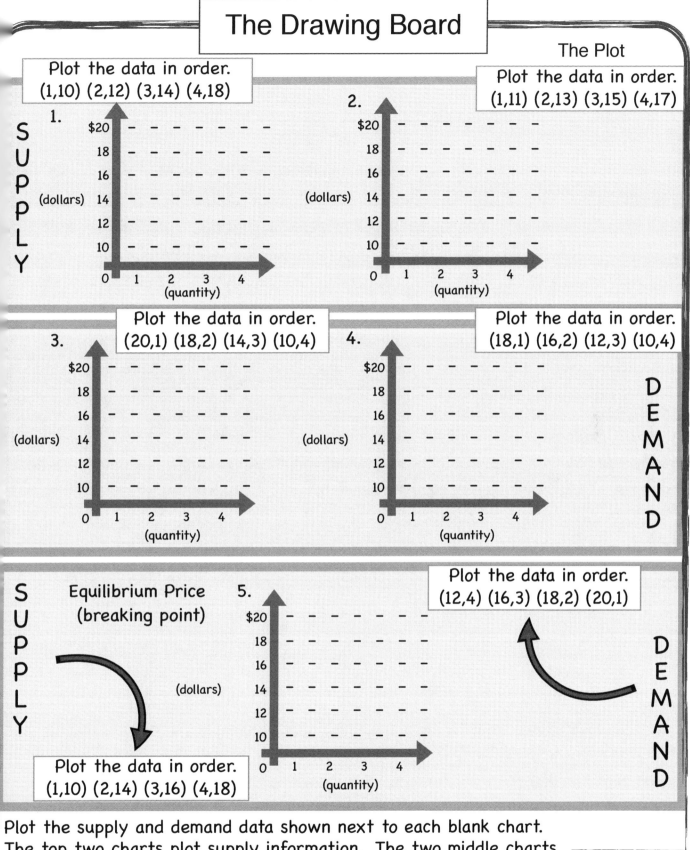

1. Plot the data in order. (1,10) (2,12) (3,14) (4,18)

SUPPLY (dollars)

2. Plot the data in order. (1,11) (2,13) (3,15) (4,17)

(dollars)

3. Plot the data in order. (20,1) (18,2) (14,3) (10,4)

(dollars)

4. Plot the data in order. (18,1) (16,2) (12,3) (10,4)

(dollars)

DEMAND

5. Plot the data in order. (12,4) (16,3) (18,2) (20,1)

SUPPLY

Equilibrium Price (breaking point)

Plot the data in order. (1,10) (2,14) (3,16) (4,18)

(dollars)

DEMAND

Plot the supply and demand data shown next to each blank chart. The top two charts plot supply information. The two middle charts plot demand information. The bottom chart will plot both supply and demand data to help Disco Roller Skates compute the equilibrium price (best product price also known as breaking point).

The Disco Roller Skates Price Will Be: $_____.

APPLY

81   www.YMBAgroup.com

Changes in the marketplace cause changes to what consumers (shoppers) buy.

Consumers respond quickly to changes in the marketplace so a business needs data to respond quickly to market changes as well.

When a company offers a product at a price much lower than the competition demand for the lower priced product will increase.

When a material needed in the production of a product becomes scarce (difficult to find) the price of the product will increase.

When a snow storm is approaching stores will quickly sell all of the shovels.

Listed below is a brief description of a decision made by either a producer or consumer. Circle who is the decision maker (producer or consumer). In the last column circle if the decision was prompted by a change in supply or a change in demand.

Decision	Decision Maker	A Change In
1. The competition just reduced their price 20%. Your company reduces the price 25%.	Producer Consumer	Supply Demand
2. Sage granite is becoming more difficult to locate, manufacturers increase the price.	Producer Consumer	Supply Demand
3. Popular history books increase $4, consumers choose to purchase less books.	Producer Consumer	Supply Demand
4. A company sells shoe laces for $20 a pair. Consumers do not purchase the product.	Producer Consumer	Supply Demand
5. Mango grape ice cream has become so popular a restaurant adds it to the menu.	Producer Consumer	Supply Demand

6. Think of a product that you or a family member recently purchased. Write the product name and approximate price below. At what price would there be less demand? At what price will consumers no longer buy the product at all?

_____

_____

_____

_____

INVESTIGATE

www.YMBAgroup.com

A company collects data to help make decisions. Data is often presented on a chart or graph. Data ready to graph is written as two numbers in parenthesis. Example: (5,12)

The first number moves sideways (left to right) along the graph. The second number will move up and down on the graph. Where the two lines intersect (cross) is the breaking point.

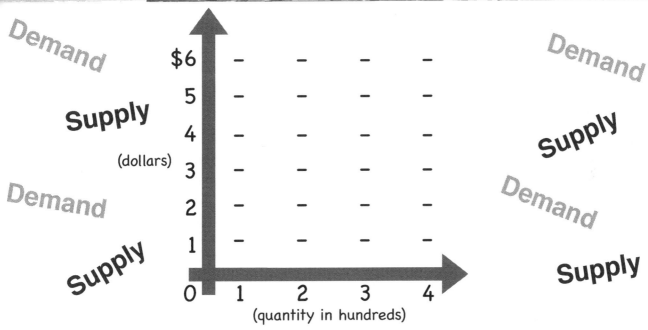

(dollars)

(quantity in hundreds)

Write the data points in parenthesis. Next, plot all eight points of data above.

SUPPLY DATA

1. 150 sell at a price of $2.00   (_____ , _____)

2. 200 sell at a price of $2.50   (_____ , _____)

3. 300 sell at a price of $3.00   (_____ , _____)

4. 350 sell at a price of $3.50   (_____ , _____)

DEMAND DATA

5. 100 are produced at a sale price of $3.50   (_____ , _____)

6. 200 are produced at a sale price of $3.00   (_____ , _____)

7. 300 are produced at a sale price of $2.50   (_____ , _____)

8. 350 are produced at a sale price of $2.00   (_____ , _____)

APPLY

Match the item from the account column to the transaction being described.

Account	Transaction
1. _____ Inventory	A. A purchase is made to stock the toys that sold last month.
2. _____ Accounts Receivable	B. The shirt printer is sent an order for five new employee shirts.
3. _____ Building	C. The company invents a new, unique product design.
4. _____ Office Supplies	D. The company purchases one case of paper.
5. _____ Uniforms	E. A new advertising sign is installed at the building entrance.
6. _____ Patents	F. A customer buys 18 items and the company gives them an invoice with net 10 terms.
7. _____ Interest Earned	G. The company completes the construction of the warehouse expansion.
8. _____ Signage	H. The company checking account receives the monthly interest deposit of $16.

STRATEGIZE

The Drawing Board

Budget Category

TOOL BOX

Inventory	Cash/Checking	Landscaping
Fuel	Office Supplies	Car Loan Payable
Uniforms	Training	Equipment

Review the purchases below. Then select the **two** budget accounts that would change as a result of the purchase transaction. Remember, each purchase will have a change in CASH, ACCOUNTS RECEIVABLE or a LOAN PAYABLE account to show how the product was paid. A second transaction for each purchase will cause a change in the total dollar balance of an asset or liability account.

(Tool Box accounts may be used more than one time.)

1. A pet store purchases 5 cash registers to use in the store and pays cash.

   Account to increase: _____   Account to decrease: _____

2. A florist purchases a new delivery van and pays with a loan from the bank.

   Account to increase: _____   Account to decrease: _____

3. A baseball team purchases 4 cases of paper and pays with a check.

   Account to increase: _____   Account to decrease: _____

4. A customer purchases 2 dozen gizmos and pays in cash.

   Account to increase: _____   Account to decrease: _____

5. A lawn mowing company purchases 12 gallons of fuel and pays with cash.

   Account to increase: _____   Account to decrease: _____

6. A craft store purchases a fork lift and pays with a check.

   Account to increase: _____   Account to decrease: _____

7. The company writes a check for an employee training class.

   Account to increase: _____

   Account to decrease: _____

   INVESTIGATE

85

The Drawing Board

Puzzle Terms

Complete the crossword puzzle below.

Each answer is an accounting or business term.

Down:

1. The opposite of buy.
3. Another word for a business.
5. The opposite of supply.
7. A statement for a purchase.

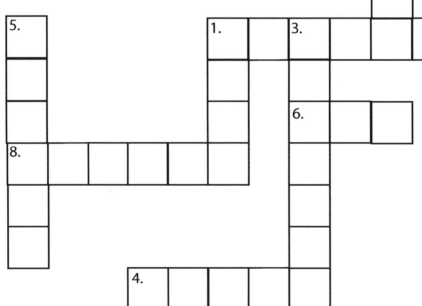

Across:

1. A company hopes a new idea will be a _____.
2. Not a service, but a _____.
4. Another name for a cent, a _____.
6. Abbreviation: Masters of Business Administration.
8. The word used in accounting for 'once a year'.

THINK

www.YMBAgroup.com

The Drawing Board

Welcome to our class. Today you are joining a corporate training class about production and efficiency. Select the word or term from the tool box to match the micro-economics topic being discussed.

The instructor says, "That brings us to the part of the day where each class member will share one production concern in their department. As a group we will brainstorm to come up with suggestions. Remember, brainstorming is when a series of ideas are discussed, but we are not yet selecting a solution.

1. I am in the marketing department. When we need only a few flyers we print them ourselves. But, our printer ink does not work well until about the 5th copy. Each time a new print job is run there are four pages we throw in the trash. The economic term being described here is: _____

2. I am in the shipping department. I am concerned about our _____. When a rush order needs to be shipped we get delayed making boxes. This causes the rush order to be delayed in being sent as soon as it is ready to ship.

3. I am in the purchasing department. The color fabric chosen for the Daisy Flower toy line is very popular. It is in such high demand the price keeps going up - and I still can not find enough to buy. The fabric chosen by the design team is so hard to locate, it is showing signs of _____. Production needs more of this _____ to continue the production of the toy.

4. I am in the management office. We noticed that when the _____ of of the Rumble Bumble Truck was lowered that the demand for the truck got very high. Consumers bought them faster than _____ could make them!

Economics Terms

TOOL BOX

Production Waste	Resource	Production
Scarcity	Price	Efficiency

APPLY

Y.M.B.A. Learning Workbook Answer Key

Page 9: answers will vary.
Page 10: answers will vary, but should contain promotion, place, price, product name.
Page 11: answers will vary.
Page 12: answers will vary but should mention a detail related to product, place, price or promotion.
Page 13: (1) poor name (2) poor idea (3) high price and poor name (4) poor name (5) poor idea (6) answers should include either poor name, high price or a poor general idea.
Page 14: answers should include a positive feature of the product update or addition.
Page 15: each of the eight items at the bottom of the page should be included on one of the eight lines at the top of the page.
Page 16: answers will vary.
Page 17: (1) good (2) both (3) service (4) good (5) good (6) both (7) good (8) both (9) both (10) service
Page 18: (1) customer will pass full price items on the way to the clearance racks. (2) answers will vary but should bring the womens and childrens items in spaces next to each other.
Page 19: box front should have a picture of the clock, a name of the product, a price and some features.
Page 20: (1) $0.75 (2) $4.95 (3) $0.99 (4)$0.95 (5) $0.49 (6) $4.95 (7) $0.99 (8) $0.75 (9) $0.89 (10) $5.55 (11) answers will vary (12) answers will vary (13) higher prices will appear lower when ending in 5 or 9.

INVESTIGATE

Page 21 Top: (1) answers should include various charity functions or services. (2) answers will vary but should include a promotion or gift of appreciation. (3) answers vary, may include fast response or lending equipment or tools. (4) answers should include tools that keep the name present such as a baseball team sponsorship, a billboard, free t-shirt give away.
Page 21 Bottom: (1) to (10) answers will vary but should include company brand names.
Page 22: (1) Circle: water, medicine, bar of soap, place to live. Underline: puppy dog, bottled water, scented shampoo, notebook with sparkle, designer medicine case, video game. (2) many shoppers would buy the luxury soap since a little more money, but an extra bar and extra quality. (3) urgent (4) urgent (5) time to shop (6) time to shop.
Page 23: answers should include: (1) an attention grabbing phrase or word (2) a promotion or limited sale would keep the buyer interest (3) rare or useful features would create buyer desire (4) a limited time or limited stock creates action.
Page 24: (1) answers will vary. (2) technology and competition cause changes in the market. (3) Unlikely due to high demand, no coupons needed to convince shoppers to buy. (4) Less demand will cause the price to go down. (5) answers will vary. (6) minimizing (7) moving, growing stage. (8) introduction entrance stage
Page 25: (1) leading (2) non-leading (3) non-leading (4) leading (5) closed (6) open (6) closed (7) open
Page 26: (1) good (2) good (3) good (4) good (5) service (6) service (7) good (8) service. Product examples sold will vary.

Page 27: answers will vary.
Page 28: (1) answers may include preparing food, bringing food the table, cleaning your table. (2) 84 (3) the large part of the business is repairing items, a service. Parts are only sold as part of the service. (4) sharks are a scary tour, need to build buyer confidence in tour guides.
Page 29:

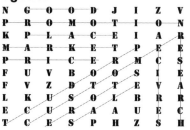

(1) retail (2) market (3) place (4) price (5) sale
Page 30:

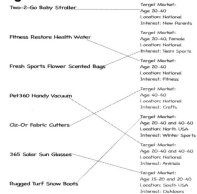

Page 31: answers will vary.
Page 32: (1) $82,000 (2) $70,500 (3) $25,500 (4) $42,400 divided by 2 since payroll is half expenses = $21,200. Next, $21,200 divided by 2 since two employees = $10,600 each
Page 33: (1) $3.00 (2) $7.19 (3) $63. (4) $13.96 (5) $47.96
Page 34: (1) Yes, sales numbers sho a small increase each year (2) payrol inventory, telephone (3) inventory, payroll (4) (a) $25,500 (b) $70,500 (c) $70,500 - $25,500 = $45,000.

Page 36:

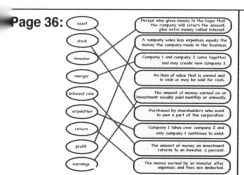

Page 37: (1) ($10x6)+($60x2)+30=60+ 120+30 = $210 (2) ($120 x 2) + $480 = $720 (3) ($60x4) + ($10x8)= $320 (4) $10+$120 = $130 (5) ($30x8) + ($480 x2) = $240 + $960 = $1,200 (6) $60 $30+$480 = $570

Page 38: graph plots should trend up and increase. (1) 4 million

Page 39: (1) false, more (2) false, money (3) false, Washington, DC (4) false, federal (5) false, does (6) false, money (7) false, law (8) false, closing (9) false, five (10) false, 1920's

Page 40:

Page 41:

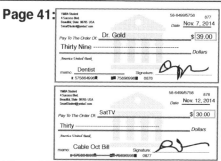

(1) and (2) see checks above.
(3) $256

Page 42: top to bottom numbers to read: 7, 6, 4, 1, 5, 3, 2.

Page 43: (1) check (2) atm (3) loan secured (4) cash (5) trade (6) loan unsecured (7) credit card (8) electronic payment

Page 44: (2) $2,000x.01 x2 = $40 (3) $4,000x.03x1=$120 (4) $800x.03x3=$72 (5)$40+$120+ $72=$232

Page 45: answers will vary. answers to 1 and 2 should not end in Co., Inc., Incorporated, Company, Corp. or Corporation. answers 3 and 4 should end in Co., Inc., Incorporated, Corp., Company or Corporation.

Page 46:

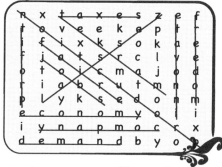

cryptogram: competition motivates a business to innovate.

Page 47: answers will vary.

Page 48: (1)$21,000 divided by 14,000=$1.50 per share. $1.50 x 1,000 shares = $1,500 (2) $12,600 divided by 3,000 = $4.20 per share. $4.20 x 20 = $84 (3) $30,000 divided by 15,000 =$2.00 per share. $2.00 x 100 = $200 (4) $16,400 divided by 8,000 = $2.05 per share. $2.05 x 400 = $820 (4) $5,250 divided by 3,000=$1.75 per share. $1.75 x 50 = $87.50

Page 49: answers will vary.

Page 50: (1) bull (2) bull (3) bear (4) bear (5) bull (6) bear (7) bear

Page 51: clockwise top left: 4, 3, 8, 9, 7, 10, 6, 2, 5, 1.

Page 52: (1) floating rate (2) junk (3) zero coupon (4) asset backed.

Page 53: answers will vary.

Page 54: (2) $850 x .04 = $34. $34 + $850 = $884. (3) ($100x12) + ($100 x 12) = $1,200 + $1,200 = $2,400 (4) ($40 x 6) + $500 = $740 (5) ($6,000 x .04)+($2,400 x .04) = $240+$96=$336

Page 55: (1) $200x.02=$4 $200+$4= $204 (2) $25x12=$300 $300x.05= $15 $300+$15=$315 (3) 52-3=49 weeks 49x$2=$98. spent half $98 divided by 2 = $49 saved. (4) $204+$315+$49=$568

Page 56: (1) approved (2) denied (3) approved (4) denied

Page 57: (1) .5, 50% (2) 1/4, 25% (3) .4, 40% (4) 3/4, .75 (5) 8/10, 80%

Page 58: (2) $500, $100, 5,$20,5, $20,5, $100, $100, $100,$20,5, 5 months plus 5 months = 10 months = 0 years 10 months. (3) $3,000,$50,60,$10,60,$10,60,$600, $600,$600,$50,12,60 months +12 months = 72 months = 6 years, zero months.

Page 59: all not correct. (1) never late (2) $2,000 (3) agency 3, 4424 (4) 2009 (5) Warren, MI

Page 60: (1) $74.95+$95+$50+$50= $269.95 (2) $34.25x12=$411 (3) $20+ $41.75+$108.40+$18.12=$187.77 (4) $5.25+$5.40+$5.50=$16.15 (5)$30x11= $330 (6) $50x2=$100 then $100 divided by 5 months = $20 a month to save.

Page 61:(1) E (2) B (3) D (4) C (5) A (6) F (7) answers will vary.

Page 62:

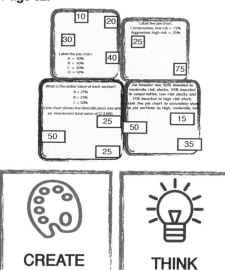

www.YMBAgroup.com

Page 64: (1) 21 (2) $12,325 (3) $862.75 (4) $12,325-$3,045=$9,280 (5) $3,625

Page 65: (1) b (2) a (3) a (4) b (5) b (6) b (7) a (8) a (9) a (10) b

Page 66: (1) 16 x $6=$96 (2) 52 x $12 =$624 (3) 214 x $2.50=$535 (4) 25 x $50=$1,250

Page 67:

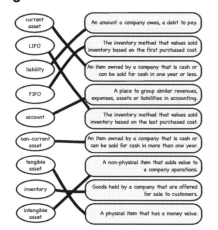

Page 68: (1) $298.53 + $25 late fee = $323.53 (2) $826.80 (3) $492.48 + $49.25 late fee =$541.73

Page 69:

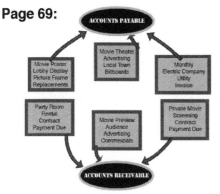

Page 70: (1) $9,000 (2) $33,900 (3) $21,600 (4) $12,400

Page 71: (1) $2,000 (2) $200 (3) $6,000 (4) $42,000 (5) $30,600 (6) $75,000 (7) $21,000 (8) $130,000 (9) $182,000 (10) $2,800 (11) $4,000 (12) $60,800 (13) $74,800

Page 72: (1) b (2) a (3) b (4) a (5) a (6) a (7) January (8) April, May, June

Page 73: (1) varies, one answer circled (2) varies, four answers circled (3) varies, answers should logically be part of the overall expense category.

Page 74: (1) answer should include that inventory is needed for the new customers.

(2) by knowing how many satisfy one zip code the company can use math to solve how many are needed for three more. (3) the current 4 employees multiplied by 3 more zip codes equals 12 new employees.

Page 75: (1) (a) machinery and bank loan (b) no change (2) (a) checking and credit card (b) decrease (3) (a) checking and accounts receivable (b) increase

Page 76: (1) increase (2) both years are $267,000 (3) more coupons and returns (4) higher prices or ordered more (5) more expenses or more coupons given (6) $288,000

Page 77: (1) increase (2) $90,000 - $78,000 = $12,000 (3) $45,000 - $40,000 = $5,000 (4) 2013 (5) $14,200 divided by 12 months = $1,183.33 (6) $40,000 divided by 2 = $20,000 (7) $90,000 divided by $9,000 = .10, as a percent 10% sales tax.

Page 78: (1) the company has little debt. (2) there is cash easily available to pay all bills. (3) the company may have difficulty paying bills since less than 2. (4) the company may pay dividends, but not a low p/e ratio so not likely high dividends.

Page 79: (1) $295,000 x .25 = $73,750 (2) $21,000+$12,000+ $24,800+$56,400+$73,750= $187,950 (3) $50 divided by $10.50=high p/e dividends high

Page 80: (1) $28/$7=$4, high p/e so high dividends if paid. (2) $44,000/$88,000=.5, low d/e so the company can easily pay bills (3) ($84,000+$4,300)/$7,700=11.48 very high quick ratio, bills easily paid (4) $250,000/$55,250=4.52, above 2 so company needs less than half of assets to pay bills.

Page 81: (1) $16 (breaking point)

Page 82: (1) producer/demand (2) producer/supply (3) consumer/ demand (4) consumer/demand (5) producer/demand (6) varies

Page 83: (1) (1.5,2) (2) (2,2.5 (3) (3,3) (4) (3.5,3.5) (5) (1,3.5) (6) (2,3) (7) (3,2.5) (8) (3.5,2)

Page 84: (1) A (2) F (3) G (4) D (5) B (6) C (7) H (8) E

Page 85: (1) office supplies/cash (2) car loan/loan payable (3) office supplies/checking (4) inventory/cash (5) fuel/cash (6) equipment/checking (7) training/checking

Page 86:
Down
(1) sell (3) company (5) demand (7) invoice
Across
(1) success (2) good (4) penny (6) MBA (8) annual

Page 87: (1) production waste (2) efficiency (3) scarcity/resource (4) price/production.

Notes:

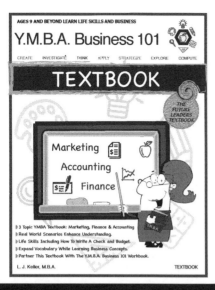
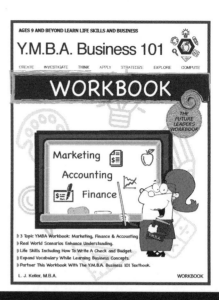

Made in the USA
Lexington, KY
13 April 2015